NEAL BASCOMB is the author of *The Race of the Century: The Battle to Break the Four-Minute Mile*, which *Kirkus Reviews* called a "gripping narrative nonfiction tale," and *The Nazi Hunters*, winner of the YALSA Award for Excellence in Nonfiction, among numerous other awards. *School Library Journal* praised his second young adult book, *Sabotage*, as "excellent" in a starred review and *The Grand Escape* as a "fantastic pick for avid history readers," also in a starred review. His book *The Racers* was named a BCCB Blue Ribbon Book, and a starred review from *School Library Journal* deemed *The Racers* "Highly Recommended." In addition, he is the author of several works of nonfiction for adults on subjects ranging from a 1905 Russian submarine mutiny to a contemporary high school robotics team. *The Perfect Mile*, *Winter Fortress*, and *Hunting Eichmann* went on to be *New York Times* and international bestsellers. Neal lives in Philadelphia with his family and rascal dog, Moses. Please visit his website at nealbascomb.com and follow him on Facebook at @nealrbascomb.

THE SALT MARCH

GANDHI'S HEROIC MARCH TO FREEDOM

NEAL BASCOMB

ILLUSTRATIONS BY MITHIL THAKER

SCHOLASTIC FOCUS
NEW YORK

Library of Congress Cataloging-in-Publication Data available

ISBN 978-93-5954-936-1

First edition, September 2024

This reprint edition, September 2024

Book design by Maithili Joshi

Printed in India at Shivam Offset Press, New Delhi

Praise for THE GRAND ESCAPE

★ "Suspenseful reading, enhanced by diagrams and photographs. A fine escapade related with proper drama and likely to be news even to well-read young historians."

—***Kirkus Reviews***, starred review

★ "It is a tale of triumph that became a template for future prisoners of war, and Bascomb's heavy, well-cited research provides the information readers need . . . A fantastic pick for avid history readers."

—***School Library Journal***, starred review

Praise for SABOTAGE

★ "Bascomb is a master of taking complicated histories and turning them into exciting works of nonfiction . . . This excellent treatise on a little-known episode of World War II is a first choice."

—***School Library Journal***, starred review

Praise and Awards for THE NAZI HUNTERS

Winner of the YALSA Award for Excellence in Nonfiction
Winner of the Sydney Taylor Book Award, Young Adult category

"From cafés in Buenos Aires to the halls of the fledgling Israeli government, from false identities to secret drops, this story has all the hallmarks of a spy novel. Bascomb has a knack for turning complex detail into a suspenseful, heart-pounding narrative."

—***School Library Journal***

"Tension rises from the pages, thanks to Bascomb's command of pacing, judicious use of quoted material, inclusion of archival photographs and strong descriptions."

—***Kirkus Reviews***

ALSO BY NEAL BASCOMB

The Grand Escape: The Greatest Prison Breakout of the 20th Century

The Nazi Hunters: How a Team of Spies and Survivors Captured the World's Most Notorious Nazi

The Race of the Century: The Battle to Break the Four-Minute Mile

The Racers: How an Outcast Driver, an American Heiress, and a Legendary Car Challenged Hitler's Best

Sabotage: The Mission to Destroy Hitler's Atomic Bomb

To Librarians, the Keepers of Truth

"You may call me a Salt Thief . . ."

—Mahatma Gandhi,
from his speech delivered on
April 26, 1930, at Chharwada, India,
which inspired the title of this book.

Stand ye calm and resolute,
Like a forest close and mute,
With folded arms, and looks which are
Weapons of an unvanquished war.

And if then the tyrants dare,
Let them ride among you there;
Slash, and stab, and maim, and hew;
What they like, that let them do.
With folded arms and steady eyes,
And little fear and less surprise,
Look upon them as they slay
Till their rage has died away:
Then they will return with shame,
To the place from which they came,
And the blood thus shed will speak
In hot blushes on their cheek:

Rise like lions after slumber
In unvanquishable NUMBER!
Shake your chains to earth, like dew
Which in sleep had fall'n on you:
YE ARE MANY—THEY ARE FEW.

Selections from
The Masque of Anarchy,
Percy Bysshe Shelley

THE SALT MARCH

GANDHI'S HEROIC MARCH TO FREEDOM

Mohandas Gandhi

Abbas Tyjabi

Kasturba Gandhi

Jawaharlal Nehru

Sarojini Naidu

Edward Frederick Lindley Wood, 1st Earl of Halifax, known as Lord Irwin

Manilal Gandhi

Chapter 1

The imperial train steamed through the early morning fog on December 23, 1929, toward New Delhi. The mist was so thick that a bystander would scarcely be able to make out the white-and-gold carriages as they rumbled over the tracks. On board was Lord Irwin, the viceroy of India, and his family, on their way to the city's central railway station. From there, they would be shuttled by car to the viceroy's recently completed official residence in the heart of the city.

At that very moment, twenty-year-old Bhagwati Vohra huddled in wait by the gray walls of a sixteenth-century fort overlooking the Jumna River, under a steep embankment over which the train would have to run. Vohra was a member of the Hindustan Socialist Republican Association, an organization that saw violence as a necessary tool to free its country from British rule. In a manifesto called "The Philosophy of the Bomb," its members vowed, "We shall have our revenge—a people's righteous revenge of the tyrant. Let cowards fall back and cringe for compromise and peace. We ask not for mercy, and we give no quarter. To Victory or Death!"

Vohra checked his watch. It was 7:30 a.m., and he knew he should soon be hearing the viceroy's train, which was scheduled to arrive at its destination, three miles away, at 7:40. Vohra held ready in his hands a remote electrical trigger. Running from the trigger was an insulated wire, shallowly buried in the ground, stretching the two hundred yards to the explosives he had placed earlier on the rail. He needed only to twitch his finger to set off the bomb.

It was almost impossible to see anything through the fog. If Vohra was to kill Irwin, as was his intention, his timing would have to be perfect. Detonate the explosives too soon, and the train would have time to stop, escaping derailment and pitching down the slope into jungle. Detonate too late, and Irwin's carriage may have already passed. Vohra would have lost his chance to strike a blow against the hated British Raj of India.

By that point, the British in one form or another had been a fixture in India for over three hundred years. On August 24, 1608, the five-hundred-ton galleon *Hector* arrived in a port on India's western shores, near Bombay. Its captain, Sir William Hawkins, was there to establish a depot on behalf of the East India Company, an entity officially chartered by the English Crown, to exploit trade in the region. The Mughal emperor, Jehangir, who ruled over one of the richest empires the world had ever known, stretching across the vast Indian subcontinent, gave Hawkins permission to do so. Jehangir had thrown wide the doors to an economy that produced a quarter of the world's goods.

As Shashi Tharoor described in his history *Inglorious Empire*, India was "the glittering jewel of the medieval world" at the time. American minister J. T. Sunderland, who long studied India as well, detailed how glittery indeed:

> *Nearly every kind of manufacture or product known to the civilized world—nearly every kind of creation of man's brain and hand, existing anywhere, and prized either for its utility or beauty—had long been produced in India. India was a far greater industrial and manufacturing nation than any in Europe or any other in Asia. Her textile goods—the fine products of her looms, in cotton, wool, linen and silk—were famous over the civilized world; so were her exquisite jewellery and her precious stones cut in every lovely form; so were her pottery, porcelains, ceramics of every kind, quality, color and beautiful shape; so were her fine works in metal—iron, steel, silver and gold.*
>
> *She had great architecture—equal in beauty to any in the world. She had great engineering works. She had great merchants, great businessmen, great bankers and financiers. Not only was she the greatest shipbuilding nation, but she had great commerce and trade by land and sea which extended to all known civilized countries. Such was the India the British found when they came.*

More East India Company ships arrived, depots expanded along the vast coastline, and profits surged from trade in tea, spices, sugar, fabric, salt, and other commodities. "Trade, not territory" was the calling card of the East India Company, and it succeeded brilliantly.

But greed, the collapse of the Mughal Empire, infighting among local rulers, and a lust for control eventually prompted the company to bring military power to bear. In 1757, General Robert Clive led 800 British soldiers and 2,220 sepoys (Indian infantrymen) through blinding rain to defeat a nawab (a sovereign Muslim ruler) and his 50,000-strong army outside the Bengal village of Plassey. Afterward, the East India Company accelerated their seizure of territories and began building an empire of their own on the subcontinent.

Within a century of arriving on its western shores, as one historian noted, "a company of traders was metamorphosed into a sovereign power, its accountants and traders into generals and governors, its warehouses into palaces, its race for dividends into a struggle for imperial authority. Without having set out to do so, Britain had become the successor to the Mughal emperors who had opened to her the doors of the subcontinent."

Using wile, duplicity, and often pitiless force, traders from the small island nation of Great Britain ruled over 320 million people of both tremendous wealth and extreme poverty, people who spoke in scores of languages, inhabited hundreds of native states, divided themselves among social castes, and practiced a variety of religions, including Hinduism, Islam, Buddhism, Jainism, Sikhism, Christianity, and more, and prayed to Vishnu, Allah, Buddha, and Jesus, among others.

A century later, in 1857, a mutiny of Indian sepoys against the East India Company led to widespread revolt against the occupiers, one fueled by steep taxes, annexation of princely states, British domination of textiles and other industries, high unemployment, and famine. Atrocities were committed on both sides, but the British displayed remarkable cruelty in their crushing of the rebellion. They wiped out whole villages, bayoneting the defenseless and even tying rebels to the mouths of cannons before firing the weapons.

The mutiny ended with the exile of the last Mughal emperor, Bahadur Shah Zafar, who was chiefly a symbolic figure at that point. In the wake of the violence, the British Parliament dismantled the East India Company and took governing control of India, establishing the British Raj (which means "rule"). The Government India Act of 1858, enacted by Parliament, codified this structure, officially making India a colony of Britain, and Queen Victoria the empress of India. Authority over this vast expanse of humanity was exercised through the Crown's appointed viceroy. At his command were roughly 2,000 members of the Indian Civil Service, predominantly individuals who had graduated from the best British schools.

The viceroy also oversaw the 10,000 British officers of the Indian Army, who were in charge of 60,000 British regular soldiers and 200,000 native troops. These were small numbers in the face of hundreds of millions of Indians, but one viceroy after another followed the same playbook that had cemented Britain's rule of

India in the first place. At its heart was the doctrine of divide and conquer.

First, the British continued to allow some princely states to exist. These states were directed by the princes but protected militarily by the British. One government report likened them to "breakwaters to the storm which would otherwise have swept over us in one great wave." Second, the British seeded dissension and anger between the large Hindu and Muslim populations to prevent a unified resistance. Third, they doled out benefits to those who served the Raj, whether as headmen in villages or other public servants. These benefits included generous salaries, influence, status, titles, and the right to land revenues. Fourth, but not least, they made false promises that the Indian people would have a say in how their country was governed by allowing consultative legislative bodies and political parties to exist.

Foremost among these parties was the Indian National Congress, formed in 1885. Populated mostly by Indian lawyers, journalists, and public servants, it was originally a moderate secular institution that met yearly to draft resolutions to reform—but not eliminate—the Raj. Its delegates primarily wanted the British to help with the pervasive poverty in India and to lessen the burden of taxes. They considered themselves the "loyal opposition" and sent their resolutions to the viceroy to consider at his discretion.

Into the twentieth century, the Indian National Congress gradually became a more nationalistic body (albeit still secular), and its members perceived India's many separate provinces and former kingdoms as a single country. And they wanted to have a much greater say in how it was governed. Some of the Congress's more strident members, like Bal Gangadhar Tilak, pushed to end willing cooperation with the British. As he said at a Congress meeting in 1902, "Though downtrodden and neglected, you must be conscious of your power of making the administration impossible if you but choose to make it so. It is you who manage the railroad and the telegraph, it is you who make settlements and collect revenues."

For some, speeches and resolutions were not enough. The British needed to go, and go now, and the Congress was not going to achieve that. In the 1890s, groups of these individuals turned to violence and other extreme measures. In 1912, a series of assassination attempts on government officials prompted the decision to move the capital of the British Raj from Calcutta, where a radical independence movement was on the rise, to Delhi. Architects from London designed a new city of wide, tree-lined avenues and classical stone buildings next to the twisting narrow lanes of the old city.

On December 23, 1912, the viceroy of India, Lord Hardinge, rode atop an elephant through a suburb of Delhi, in a ceremonial procession marking the transfer of the capital. Revolutionaries threw a bomb in his path, and he was lucky to survive the attack. Now, eighteen years to the day after that assassination attempt, construction was completed on the new viceregal palace, Viceroy's

House, in New Delhi. An official opening ceremony was planned for that very day—as was another bombing.

Aboard the train, in the fifth carriage from the locomotive, Lord Irwin was seated beside his wife, daughter, and several key staff members. He had a good deal on his mind. Edward Frederick Lindley Wood, 1st Earl of Halifax, known as Lord Irwin, was a member of an old, respectable family from York in northern England. His people had the good fortune to own land that was veined with coal, and at the start of the Industrial Revolution, they suddenly found themselves fabulously rich. When Edward was born, in 1881, it was without a left hand. Doctors later fitted him with a prosthetic in the shape of a clenched fist. Despite his handicap, he avidly participated in sports and riding horses.

Tragically, he lost all three of his older brothers to the scourge of disease. "All my hopes and joy are bound up in you," his father wrote to him, burdening a young Edward with tremendous expectations. Schooled at Eton, then at Oxford, Edward lived up to those expectations through hard work and upstanding morals. Wealthy, smart, well connected, and well married, there seemed no limit to his success. However, his political career always seemed to fall short of his rival and contemporary, the dynamo Winston Churchill.

As viceroy of India, Irwin had hoped to make his mark and to serve his country well. However, now into his third year in the role, he had made scarce progress in taming the Indian people's resistance against the British. Irwin feared that India was already on the verge of a major revolt. On that morning's agenda, after the formal opening ceremony for Viceroy's House, was a meeting with a group of leading Indian political figures, among them Mohandas Gandhi—or, as many of his countrymen called him, "the Mahatma" (Great Soul). Irwin aimed to lower any expectations these Indian nationalists might have of their country obtaining "dominion status," the state of autonomy within the British Commonwealth enjoyed by Canada and Australia, any time soon.

No doubt it would be a tough conversation, one made even tougher by the fact that there was no single unified approach toward India even from his own government. Tensions were rife between conservatives and liberals in Parliament over how much political power to cede to Indians, to say nothing of rival visions among British officials in Delhi and among the various provincial governments. The viceroy had to navigate all these competing currents.

Lord Irwin heard a dull boom. He thought there must have been an explosion and put down the book he was reading. Then there was a shudder throughout the carriage, followed by a drift of smoke. Clearly, somewhere, a bomb had detonated. Screams of terror erupted, and a military officer ran toward him.

Moments before, when Bhagwati Vohra triggered the detonator, the dining car had just passed over the rail to which the bomb was attached. The explosion tore through the corridor between the dining car and the third carriage, where a team of stenographers were working. The floorboards in the passageway mushroomed upward, and the heavy plate-glass windows in the adjoining carriages shattered. A sleeper compartment splintered into pieces. Amazingly, nobody was seriously injured in the initial blast. The bomb also carved a two-foot gap in the railroad track. By a stroke of good fortune—or God's hand, as the religious Irwin likely believed—the wheels of one carriage after the next jumped the gap in the rail, keeping the train, and its many passengers, from careening off the side of the severe slope. Onward the viceroy's train continued through the fog, and Vohra made his escape before the police arrived on the scene.

At New Delhi's central railway station, Lord Irwin stepped down from his carriage, shook hands with the officials awaiting him on the platform, and folded his six-foot-five frame into an idling car. "Lucky no harm had been done," he declared to reporters, playing down the assassination attempt. As King George V's representative in India, he could not appear shaken by what the British press were to call "a dastardly outrage" in their reports, particularly at the very time Indian nationalists were calling for independence.

Right on schedule, Irwin's car pulled up at the bottom of the steep white steps leading to the new Viceroy's House, where an honor guard of mounted horsemen in scarlet-and-gold uniforms stood at attention. Time to get on with the business at hand.

Chapter 2

Later that same day, Mohandas Gandhi also arrived at New Delhi's central station by train but traveling aboard a crowded carriage in third class. At sixty years of age, Gandhi made for a startling figure amid the more urbane crowd. He was wrapped in a shawl of stark white homespun cloth called khadi that left bare most of his arms and legs, and he wore round steel-rimmed glasses and sandals. He had knotty feet; short, narrow legs; bulbous knees; a thin waist; a slight, rounded chest; a heron's neck; a large shaven head, temples threaded with veins; a thick nose; toothless gums; ears that looked like they might spring into flight; and eyes that could be one moment soft, then fierce.

On the platform, Gandhi was greeted by well-wishers before a car whisked him away to meet the viceroy at Viceroy's House. Gandhi was in hopeful spirits, but given that he still had a few hours left in his weekly practice of twenty-four hours of silence, he kept his thoughts to himself. Like Lord Irwin, he had much to consider about the state of Indian affairs, especially after learning about the failed assassination attempt. Gandhi was horrified by it and knew as well as Irwin that violence would only breed more violence.

The two leaders had met just once before. In October 1927, Gandhi broke off a speaking tour of the Indian countryside to travel 1,250 miles to sit down with the viceroy, who had invited him at short notice. Irwin simply handed Gandhi a government memo that informed him the British Parliament was putting together a commission led by Sir John Simon to investigate the conditions in India and suggest political reforms. All its members would be white and British, with no Indians invited to join the commission.

The meeting ended soon after it began. If the viceroy wanted Gandhi's support for the commission, he did not get it. Gandhi thought Irwin a "good man" with no power to champion any changes in the Raj that the British prime minister and Parliament did not want to make. Further, he found Irwin unwilling to listen to any views outside of his own. For his part, the viceroy considered Gandhi impractical and "rather like talking to someone who had stepped off another planet." Instead of debating politics or the divide between Hindus and Muslims, Gandhi discussed the importance of Indians relying on khadi rather than imported British cloth to realize their self-sufficiency.

An uproar followed reports of the commission's foundation, and in February 1928, Indians across the country came out to protest the arrival of the commission's members, with black flags and calls of "Go back, Simon." As historian Louis Fischer wrote, "Indians were being treated as 'natives'; the whites would come, look around, and decide the fate of the dumb, brown Asiatics." Almost every faction of the Indian political realm was incensed.

After the Simon Commission began its work, there were calls by the Congress, particularly from its younger members, to push hard for independence. In late May 1928, a conference attended by members from the country's various political groups gathered together. Led by Motilal Nehru, twice president of the Congress, a committee was formed to draft a constitution for a free India.

Almost three months later, the *Nehru Report* outlined a constitution based on a federalized democratic system. Later that same year, the Congress passed a resolution giving the British one year to enact the independent constitution into law or risk a major protest movement that would shut down the country. When Gandhi arrived in New Delhi on December 23, 1929, that deadline was fast approaching. Irwin had muddied the waters only two months earlier by inviting Gandhi and other Indian nationalist leaders to London for a Round Table Conference in 1930. The Indian leaders took this invitation to mean that, at the very least, dominion status was on the table for discussion. Key members of the British government, including Winston Churchill, stomped on any such hopes. Thus, Gandhi had agreed to this last-minute meeting with Lord Irwin to understand and clarify the true position of his government.

At 4:00 p.m., Gandhi arrived at Viceroy's House. Standing atop a hill, it was a 340-room colossus of pink-and-cream sandstone designed by the renowned British architect Edwin Lutyens. On his approach, Gandhi passed grand sculptures of lions and elephants. Everywhere there were pools, fountains, and expanses of gardens. At the center of the palace structure rose an enormous copper dome that looked like it might float away into the blue sky. Inside, there were halls wide and tall enough to carry an echo. Marble columns, glass chandeliers, gold trim, and filigreed wood-paneled walls abounded. Thus was the treasure of India spent.

Among those accompanying Gandhi were Motilal Nehru and Muhammad Ali Jinnah, leader of the All India Muslim League, a party that had been formed in 1906 to represent Muslim interests on the Indian subcontinent, where 75 percent of the population was Hindu. Gandhi broke his weekly vow of silence only shortly before the meeting began, so his fellow nationalist leaders still had little insight into whether he was willing to attend the Round Table Conference.

The gathering, located in one of the palace's many grand chambers, was the first official meeting to be held there. First, Gandhi and the others expressed their horror at the attack on Lord Irwin. The viceroy appreciated their sentiment and quickly turned the conversation to negotiating what it would take for the nationalist leaders to come to London. Gandhi interrupted. He stated that they should first discuss the "general picture of the Indian political situation." As one of the leading lights of Indian politics, there were few better to give it.

Mohandas Karamchand Gandhi was born on October 2, 1869, in Porbandar, a town of white limestone buildings, on a peninsula that jutted out into the Arabian Sea in what is the present-day state of Gujarat in India. He was the fourth child of a middle-class Hindu family. His father served as an administrative official for the small princely state in which they lived. His mother was a housewife and profoundly religious. A shy, sensitive, middling student throughout his childhood, there was little to indicate that Mohandas would do more than follow his father into state service.

Following the custom of the time, he was married at thirteen years of age to Kasturba, the daughter of a local merchant and family friend. Like all teenagers, Gandhi had his rebellions—eating goat meat (forbidden by his religion), stealing from his older brother, contradicting his teachers, neglecting his elders—but he suffered an outsize sense of guilt and self-recrimination after each such transgression. Clearly the moral uprightness of his parents had made a deep impression on him.

After graduating from high school, he attended college, yet again struggling through his classes. If Gandhi was to have any future, a family friend suggested, he should study in London to become a lawyer. With funds from his brother and vows to his mother that he would not "touch wine, women, or meat," Gandhi departed for England in 1888. Not yet eighteen years old, he left behind his wife and newborn son.

In London, Gandhi took to wearing suits, starched white shirts, and a top hat—the height of fashion for young men at that time. He improved his English, learned French and Latin, and studied physics and common law. He kept a fastidious budget, walked ten miles a day, became a devout vegetarian, read widely, and, almost three years later, easily passed the bar exam to become a lawyer. It was a lonely period for him, and he returned to India as soon as he could.

Back home, he floundered as a novice lawyer, too timid to speak in the courtroom, left to drafting legal documents. In 1892, eager for a better job, he packed his bags again, this time for South Africa, to represent the cousin of a shipping merchant he knew from his hometown. He suspected that he would return to India in less than a year, so Kasturba and his now two children, Harilal and Manilal, stayed behind.

Advancing his career was Gandhi's principal intent in traveling to South Africa. The politics of colonialism was the furthest thing from his mind—as was the associated issue of race relations. At the time, there were hundreds of thousands of Indians in South Africa, many having come as indentured laborers. Their religion, education, caste, or job made no difference to their status. The ruling whites viewed all Indians as inferiors, calling them racist terms like "coolies" or "Asiatics." Laws restricted their movement within the country, their ability to do business, and their right to vote. Prejudice was pervasive.

Shortly after his arrival in South Africa, Gandhi was on a train from Durban to Pretoria to work on a case. He was dressed in a frock coat, well-cut pants, and a black turban, and he was seated in the first-class carriage. At one station, a white passenger objected to

occupying the same space as Gandhi, whom he openly called a coolie. The passenger summoned two railway officials to get rid of him. When they appeared, the officials ordered Gandhi to move to the lowest-class berths. Gandhi did not budge. He had paid for a first-class ticket. The officials threatened to call a police constable. "You may," Gandhi said. "I refuse to get out voluntarily." Moments later, a constable grabbed Gandhi's hand and threw him from the train. His luggage followed soon after onto the dirt.

Humiliated and enraged, Gandhi dusted himself off and spent

the night in the train station, shivering from the cold. Should he just return to Durban and go back to India, he wondered. Should he finish his case first? Should he try to address this injustice with the railway? Should he allow this place, this government, this country, to mistreat people with brown skin? The following morning, he sent a flurry of telegrams to the railway's general manager and to his boss in Durban. He explained, in no uncertain terms, that he had a valid first-class ticket and that there was no rule or law forbidding him from being seated there. The railway relented, and the stationmaster even accompanied Gandhi on board his train to make sure he had no further trouble.

Gandhi spent the next two decades of his life in South Africa, and over that time he completely transformed himself. After that haphazard rebellion over a train ticket, he became a successful lawyer and an outspoken leader of the Indian community. More important, he began what he would later call his "experiments with truth" to bring about a spiritual awakening. He was inspired most of all by his close readings of the Bhagavad Gita (or "Song of God"), one of the most important, widely read Hindu texts.

Part of a larger work, the Mahabharata, the Gita presents the tale of Prince Arjuna, who confronts his family, teachers, elders, and brothers on the battlefield, and at first, he resists the call to war. As historian Lisa Trivedi summarized, "His charioteer is an incarnation of Lord Vishnu, a figure around which many of the Hindu faith direct their devotion. Vishnu engages Arjuna in a discussion of moral duty, the necessity of facing injustice, and how the only way to become closer to the divine is to perform one's duty as Heaven requires. For Arjuna, a warrior prince, his role in society is to fight."

From the Gita, Gandhi took to heart many of the text's tenets of a life properly lived. Among them was also the concept of "selfless action." Following suit, Gandhi began to renounce material possessions and to constrain his human desires. He took to cutting his own hair, emptying his own chamber pot, handling his own laundry, tending his own maladies, simplifying his diet, and embracing a celibate life—even after his wife and family came to join him.

This ascetic existence was deepened after Gandhi read John Ruskin's *Unto This Last*, which recommended the shedding of all riches and suggested that money was a means to rule over other people. Ruskin argued, "A laborer with a spade serves society as truly as a lawyer with a brief, and the life of labor, of the tiller of the soil, is the life worth living." Soon after devouring the text, Gandhi established a communal settlement, eventually replacing his British attire for simple homemade clothes common to those worn by peasants.

In seeking equality for Indians in South Africa, Gandhi gradually developed a resistance method that was simple and that worked. Historians Peter Ackerman and Jack DuVall characterized the technique well in their book, *A Force More Powerful*. "Declare opposition to an unjust law, break the law, and suffer the consequences. Resisters' calm and dignified suffering would open the eyes of oppressors and weaken the hostility behind repression; rather than adversaries being bullied to capitulate, they would be obliged to see what was right, and that would make them change their minds and actions."

Gandhi came to call this method satyagraha. This was the merging of the Hindu word for "truth" and "holding firmly"—or in other words, "truth force." In South Africa, he developed satyagraha into a very effective tool for changing the government's laws, especially when resistance efforts not only opened "the eyes of the oppressor" but also imperiled their interests if they refused to capitulate.

As Gandhi wrote in 1909, he had met enough people of different faiths—Muslim, Hindu, Jain, Christian, Parsi, and more—to realize that "religions are different roads converging to the same point. What does it matter that we take different roads so long as we reach the same goal?" Practicing ahimsa (roughly, "not causing harm to other living things") sprung from this same idea. If truth was many-sided, then nobody should be able to compel others through violence to change their own concept of it. The Hindu, Buddhist, and Jainist faiths all had deep underpinnings in the principle of ahimsa, or what we might call nonviolence. So too did the Bible's Sermon on the Mount as well as the writings of Leo Tolstoy. Gandhi read and absorbed all of these.

It was a short step to reach the conclusion that using violence to end repression was a morally bankrupt position—and also ineffective. Terrorism or riots or destruction of property only bred more fear, more oppression, more prejudice. As Gandhi wrote about affecting political change: "The means may be likened to a seed, the end to a tree . . . We reap what we sow."

In January 1915, Gandhi returned to India to take up the fight to improve the rights of his own compatriots under the British Raj. It did not take long for him to become the leader of this movement.

Now, in Viceroy's House, after a half-hour-long history of why the Indian people had good cause to distrust their British occupiers, Gandhi stiffly explained that he would not attend the 1930 Round Table Conference unless there was a commitment on immediate dominion status. This declaration took most in the room by surprise. Irwin made the point that the conference was being assembled precisely to discuss these issues of self-government. There was a chance, he said, "of doing something big" if Gandhi and the others came to London. Otherwise, they risked missing out on a great opportunity.

Gandhi was unmoved. He needed some proof that Britain was willing to relinquish power before he agreed to come. Others could go, but he would not. It was left unsaid, but he was clearly convinced that the British would never withdraw from India as a result of talks alone. They needed their hand to be forced.

After less than two hours, the meeting ended, without any resolution. Gandhi and Motilal Nehru left straightaway for the train station. They faced an overnight journey to the city of Lahore, the capital of the Punjab, where the Indian National Congress was gathering for its annual session. All eyes now turned on Lahore, in expectation of what would come next.

In the northwest of India, crowned by the Himalayas, the Punjab province (along with Bengal and Bombay) was a hotbed of the independence movement. Shortly before Gandhi and Motilal Nehru's arrival, a thunderstorm caused the banks of the Ravi River to overflow, leaving the ground a muddy soup. After the downpour, frigid temperatures and blustery winds settled over the city of Lahore. Congress delegates, including Gandhi, were afflicted with the cold. Encamped in tents on the riverbank, they slept on little more than beds of straw and were barely warmed by their charcoal stoves and wool shawls. Crackling frost covered the ground at night, and in the mornings their food had to be thawed out before it could be eaten. Even the juicy flesh of the oranges Gandhi had brought with him from New Delhi had frozen solid.

On December 25, Jawaharlal Nehru arrived by train into Lahore's central station. The forty-year-old son of Motilal Nehru and protégé of Gandhi, Jawaharlal was the newly elected president of the Congress. Educated at Cambridge University, he was a lawyer by vocation and—at first impression—lacked the air of a revolutionary. He had a boyish face, dressed neatly, spoke even more neatly, and had the vulnerable look of a poet. But rooted inside him was a drive to free his people from the chains of the British Raj. No doubt this desire was fostered by his father, as was Jawaharlal's conviction that he was destined to do great things. He had hesitated to accept the Congress presidency, but Gandhi persuaded him that the urgency of youth was required, now more than ever.

When Nehru got off the train, he was surrounded by well-wishers who garlanded him with flowers and shouted, "Long live the

Revolution!" It took an hour just to get clear of the station. Several days after his arrival, his opening of the forty-fourth annual session of the Indian National Congress was no less celebratory. He rode a white horse from the river encampment to the enormous pandal (a temporary tentlike structure) where the session was being held. Over fifty thousand people had come to Lahore for the gathering, and expectations were high. The time for talk was over. The year of grace that the Congress had given the British government to enact a constitution for India based on the *Nehru Report* would end on New Year's Day. The crowds held aloft banners that carried messages like "World Peace Depends on India's Freedom."

In his speech opening the session, Nehru declared that dominion status for India was no longer sufficient. "Independence means for us complete freedom from British domination," he said. "There is now an open conspiracy to free the country from foreign rule." Nehru signaled for the Congress flag to be raised, and the horizontal triband of saffron, white, and green with a charka (spinning wheel) in the center was unfurled sixty feet high on its flagpole.

On December 31, it was Gandhi's turn to take to the podium to argue for a resolution that clearly stated their goal: purna swaraj. Complete independence from Britain. To achieve swaraj, Gandhi declared, acts like the "bomb outrage on the viceregal train" must never be their method. Such terrorism only harmed their cause. They were going to follow a campaign of civil disobedience. Some of those present pushed back, arguing that nonviolent protests would never prompt the British to relinquish their hold on India.

Physical force could only be met with physical force. Gandhi swayed the majority otherwise.

At one minute after midnight, Congress passed the resolution calling for purna swaraj and a civil disobedience campaign to realize it. Then there was dancing, singing of the national anthem, and shouts of "Inquilab Zindabad" ("Long live the Revolution") into the early hours of the morning. Nehru may have been the one who spurred forward the idea of independence, but it was clear that Gandhi would be the general of any campaign to achieve it.

Chapter 3

On the overnight train journey from Lahore to his home outside Ahmedabad, an industrial city in western India, Gandhi thought a lot about violence. He was drafting an essay in response to the attack on Lord Irwin. Many at the Congress meeting had asked him how he was going to avoid the pair of violent events, Jallianwala Bagh and Chauri Chaura, that bookended the years 1919 to 1922, when he first played a major national role in India's politics. Those two disasters were permanently marked in Gandhi's mind, and for the past decade he had continuously asked himself the same question.

At the end of World War I, in February 1919, the viceroy—Lord Chelmsford at the time—had passed the Rowlatt Act. Its official name was the Anarchical and Revolutionary Crimes Act of 1919. Most Indians referred to it as the Black Acts. It instituted a set of harsh laws that included press restrictions, indefinite detentions, and trials without juries. Chelmsford's move was deeply unpopular, with Gandhi foremost. At the time, Gandhi was just finding his feet in India after two decades fighting for the rights of Indian immigrants in South Africa. In protest against the Rowlatt Act, Gandhi called for a national hartal (general strike) across India. His first major political act against the Raj, the hartal was a bold move and captured the imagination of the people.

On April 6, 1919, Gandhi stood in front of a boisterous crowd of 150,000 in Bombay and declared the start of the strike. Grocers shuttered their shops. Factories closed. Docks emptied of workers. The strike paralyzed numerous cities. Instead of participating in an economy that filled British coffers, Indians gathered in the streets or returned home to fast and to pray.

A few days later, Gandhi was briefly detained on his way to the Punjab. In response, protests against the British broke out across India. Most were peaceful, but some escalated into throwing stones, burning buildings, and assaulting British citizens. In Ahmedabad, troops fired on rioters, killing twenty-three people. Horrified, Gandhi fasted for three days in penance and declared the hartal a "Himalayan miscalculation." He urged volunteers to take a pledge of nonviolence and to resist the temptation to loot, riot, and stage large demonstrations that might break out into violence.

But events were already out of his control. In the Punjab, a crowd raged through the ancient city of Amritsar to protest the arrest by local forces of the city's political leaders. Several British banks were torched, three bank managers were killed, and the headmistress of a local girls' school, Marcella Sherwood, was grieviously assaulted. Brigadier General Reginald Dyer, charged with keeping the peace, ordered a ban on assemblies or meetings, including worshipping at mosques and temples.

On April 13, 1919, demonstrators defied the law by gathering in an enclosed garden called the Jallianwala Bagh, not far from the Golden Temple, the most sacred site of the Sikh religion. Since it was market day, the square was crowded with many of the city's residents going about their normal day. Nonetheless, Dyer stationed his troops at the narrow entrances to the garden,

corralling everyone inside. Then Dyer took it upon himself to produce "a sufficient moral effect" (as he later explained) by killing as many people as he could. He ordered his soldiers to open fire on the penned-in, defenseless crowd.

The only escape from the barrage of bullets was a well in the center of the square. Many pitched themselves into the well, falling to their deaths. By the time the guns fell silent, there were 1,137 wounded and 379 dead. Two days later, Dyer's effort to teach the

"Asiatic" a lesson still incomplete, he had several rebel leaders publicly flogged, and he forced any Indian who passed Miss Sherwood's school to crawl on all fours like an animal. Those who refused were dragged by his troops to a pole and whipped.

Reports about the massacre and its aftermath only slowly escaped the city due to the Raj's coordinated blackout of news. When Gandhi learned of it, his faith in the British to act justly—or with restraint—was lost. Still, he wavered over what to do. Many within the Indian National Congress demanded immediate action.

Instead, Gandhi took a step back from politics and focused his attention on promoting khadi. It seemed like an odd pursuit, but Gandhi believed that revitalizing handicrafts like homespun and home-woven cloth, which had been decimated by machine-made British goods, would advance the self-reliance of the Indian people. In his view, self-reliance was critical for them to establish self-rule. Leading by example, he and his ashramites began spinning cotton on hand-cranked wheels (charkas) or a simple handle spindle (takli) to produce a daily quota of yarn that could then be woven into khadi.

Over the next couple of years, Gandhi gradually stepped back into politics, mixing social reforms like education and improving Hindu-Muslim relations with increasing talk of another noncooperation campaign against the British. He raised money and all but took control of the Congress. Finally, on July 31, 1921, he launched another nationwide movement to withdraw from involvement with the British. Indians boycotted their goods and picketed liquor shops. (Gandhi believed alcohol an evil.) They quit their jobs in the civil service, legislatures, and courts. Teachers and students alike abandoned schools; and many Indians stopped paying taxes. Lord Chelmsford, the viceroy, responded by censoring the press and targeting the campaign's leadership for arrest.

As before, events moved beyond Gandhi's control. On February 4, 1922, in the town of Chauri Chaura in the United Provinces, northeast India, the police tried to disperse protesters by firing warning shots over their heads. Memories of the Jallianwala Bagh massacre were still fresh, and the crowd—some of whom had earlier sworn nonviolence—became enraged. They chased the policemen into the town hall and set the building on fire, all the while screaming, "Victory to Mahatma Gandhi." Twenty-three died in the inferno.

After this savagery, Gandhi immediately suspended the civil disobedience campaign, stopped his constant travels, and retreated to his ashram. Many within the Indian National Congress (notably, Motilal Nehru) and the Muslim League (notably, Muhammad Ali Jinnah) were stunned—and upset—over the sudden calling off of the movement, particularly without their consultation. A week later, Gandhi was arrested for publishing seditious material in his newspaper *Young India*. He pleaded guilty. "Noncooperation with evil is as much a duty as is cooperation with the good," he said at his trial. The British judge sentenced Gandhi to six years in jail.

While serving his time, Gandhi pledged not to relaunch any campaign for India's freedom until its people were ready. In 1924, the

British government decided to release Gandhi before his sentence was complete. Gandhi returned straightaway to his work, this time fighting for a different kind of independence: the independence of the soul of every Indian. "I am not interested in freeing India merely from the English yoke. I am bent upon freeing India from any yoke whatsoever," he said.

In practical terms, this meant two things. First, casting off their colonizer's way of life—whether it be the clothes, diet, or obsession with making money—to follow a more ascetic life, as Gandhi had done. Second, ridding Indian society of its many "defects," including the mistreatment of Untouchables (the lowest rung in the strict Hindu social hierarchy, which was determined by birth), the marriage of children, the lack of sanitation, and more. Until you rule yourself, Gandhi believed, you would never be free. First and foremost, swaraj meant self-rule.

When speaking to a crowd, he would raise his left hand in a fist. Then, unpeeling one finger at a time, he pointed out the five requirements for true Indian freedom: (1) equality for the Untouchables; (2) devotion to khadi; (3) abstinence from alcohol and opium; (4) peace between Hindus and Muslims; and (5) equality for women. By pursuing these aims, Gandhi believed, India would cleanse itself of weakness, and its people would be all the more ready to fight for independence from Britain.

Gandhi made substantial strides in this five-pronged noncooperation campaign. His countrymen revered him for it. But the assassination attempt on Lord Irwin by Bhagwati Vohra and the

Hindustan Socialist Republican Association signaled to Gandhi that he must tread carefully. The cauldron of rage that had boiled over at Jallianwala Bagh and Chauri Chaura would be stirred up once more if he chose the wrong course of action. By the time his train arrived in Ahmedabad, Gandhi had finished his essay, titled "The Cult of the Bomb," in which he emphasized that violence against the British would only bring more suffering and more violence. The Raj would never back down in the face of it. Mass civil disobedience, he argued, offered the only path to freedom. Now all he needed was to figure out exactly what form that civil disobedience should take.

Gandhi's community, located just outside Ahmedabad alongside the Sabarmati River, was named the Satyagraha Ashram. He had started the ashram with his wife in 1917. It was a peaceful place. There was a scattering of simple houses, many with covered terraces. It had a kitchen and dining hall, prayer grounds and playgrounds, a school and a library, gardens and utility sheds, and open-air rooms where the inhabitants could spin cotton into khadi yarn or run the printing press. Tamarind trees offered shade from the fierce sun, and wild monkeys roamed the site's expansive grounds.

Home to Gandhi, his family, and over 250 devoted supporters, the ashram was both a refuge and a base of operations for Gandhi's reform movements, his continuing "experiments with truth." In January 1930, Gandhi's son Manilal was living there in a spartan room he shared with his wife, Sushila, and their newborn daughter, Sita. After many years in South Africa, where he had run his father's newspaper, the *Indian Opinion*, thirty-seven-year-old Manilal was glad to be back in India. Sushila had wanted to come too, eager to introduce her family to their first child. Their arrival in December was good timing. Manilal was able to attend the annual session of the Indian National Congress in Lahore, as a representative of the South African Indian Congress. Now their short visit to India looked like it might last much longer. With the promised nonviolent campaign ahead, Manilal was eager to participate in any way he could.

What shape that campaign would take preoccupied his father throughout January. Visitors and letters offering advice poured into the ashram. The poet and nationalist leader Sarojini Naidu came and sat with Gandhi as he spun cotton on his charka, listening to him tell her about how he had labored to find a light in the darkness. Fifty-one-year-old Naidu was a slight figure with bright, intelligent eyes. In 1925, she was elected the Indian National Congress president, the first woman elevated to that position. A world-famous writer as well, known as the "Nightingale of India," she preferred her colorful silk saris and jewels to the white, loosely bound khadi garments and triangular-shaped "Gandhi caps" that others wore. Only recently, she had been in America, where she spoke to packed halls about Indian independence. Now she urged Gandhi to include women in any campaign.

Jawaharlal Nehru, in his frequent visits to the ashram and in his letters to Gandhi, promoted a big sweeping action. "For myself, I delight in warfare," Nehru once wrote. Others, like moderates Satyendra Bose, preached caution, pleading with Gandhi to restart negotiations with Lord Irwin instead of launching a civil disobedience campaign. Muslim leaders, like Shaukat Ali, also pushed against any action, chiefly because the Congress had largely excluded them from any decision-making about fighting the government.

Through it all, Gandhi weighed the possibilities and listened for his "inner voice" to steer him on the right course. One option available to him was a national strike. This might attract a lot of attention and inflict damage on the Raj, but how was he to sustain it? More important, how would he prevent it from escalating into violent confrontation, as had happened in Amritsar or Chauri Chaura? On the other hand, even a nonviolent campaign might trigger violence anyway. In the wake of the Wall Street Crash, India was suffering from the same economic depression as the rest of the world, and the working class was ripe for rebellion if nonviolence failed to bring about significant change.

Further, he needed something more than just to strike against the British Raj: He needed a way to teach the power of satyagraha, thereby strengthening the Indian masses so that they were ready for full independence. Whatever they decided to do, the campaign had to feel like it was led by the people, from the poorest upward, rather than a political gambit of the leadership of the Indian National Congress.

Manilal knew that his father would make the decision by himself and that there would be no vote. All he could do now was what he had always done, and that was to support his father—ever the faithful son. As part of that commitment, Manilal and his young family embraced the principles of the Satyagraha Ashram, where all residents were treated as equals, regardless of caste, sex, religion, nationality, age, or familial closeness to Bapu (an affectionate and intimate Gujarati term for "father"), which is what they all called Gandhi.

At the ashram, everyone lived as brothers and sisters. They dined together, worked together, and prayed together. Nobody was exempt from duties, including Gandhi himself, whether that was tending the gardens, cooking meals, caring for the children, washing dishes, or cleaning the latrines. The schedule and restrictions were no less rigid. The day was divided into three parts. Eight hours for rest and sleep. Eight hours for personal well-being, including eating, exercise, bathing, and keeping a diary. And, finally, eight hours for social service, including physical labor and morning and evening prayers. All ashramites spun and wore khadi and observed a vegetarian diet and a vow of poverty.

Manilal understood the discipline of the ashram well. He had lived it ever since he was a young boy at Phoenix Settlement, his family's home in South Africa. If anything, he thought Bapu had calmed since those days. Manilal remembered much harsher regimes and a lack of forgiveness there. Once, he forgot to bring his glasses to work at his father's office, and Gandhi demanded his son march five miles home on his own to fetch them, then the five miles back again—all to teach him to mind his things better. He was barely twelve. No doubt Manilal knew that the moment was fast approaching when this strict discipline would be needed to follow where his father planned to lead them.

On January 26, 1930, as had been decided at Lahore, India's first independence day was celebrated across the subcontinent. At the ashram on the banks of the Sabarmati River, the Congress tricolor was raised on a flagpole, and each of Gandhi's ashramites took the pledge: "We believe that it is the inalienable right of the Indian people, as of any other people, to have freedom and to enjoy the fruits of their toil." Celebrations and singing continued through the night. Throughout India, hundreds of thousands took the same pledge, vowing to work for their freedom. There were no indications of violence. The peaceful, enthusiastic response to the day encouraged Gandhi that the time was ripe for nonviolent civil disobedience.

Lord Irwin's response to the declaration of independence soon followed. He gave no commitment to offering dominion status and called the wave of independence pledges nothing more than "stage lightning and teapot thunder." In one speech, he declared, "Independence will bring India irreparable misfortune and disaster." In another, he threatened, "I shall discharge to the full the responsibility resting upon myself and upon my government for the effective maintenance of the authority of law."

Gandhi returned with his own statement, published in *Young India*. He offered the British one last chance to avoid a campaign of civil disobedience if they instituted eleven points of reform, including the establishment of protective tariffs against British cloth, the prohibition of alcohol, elimination of the oppressive Criminal Investigation Department, massive cuts in military and civil service salaries, a 50 percent reduction in land taxes, and the abolition of the salt tax. Gandhi admitted that the list of demands was a "childish offer," since the Raj was unlikely to accept it, but he offered it nonetheless in the spirit of cooperation.

He was still racking his mind, night and day, well into the first week of February, over what would be the first action in their campaign. Suggestions flowed into the ashram. March on New Delhi and occupy the Red Fort or Viceroy's House. Institute a nationwide strike. Stop paying taxes. None of them seemed right. Slowly, inspiration came to Gandhi. There was no epiphany. No thunderbolt or light bulb. Rather, an idea slowly took form in his thoughts. Although at first he kept it to himself, his confidence in the plan grew daily.

On February 15, leading Congress members gathered at the ashram to hear whether Gandhi had settled on an idea. Sarojini Naidu was as eager as anyone assembled on the top floor of the main ashram building to learn the focus of their civil disobedience campaign. "Salt," Gandhi said. They would focus their nonviolent campaign entirely on the abolition of the salt tax. Like her fellow Congress members, Naidu was flabbergasted. *Salt?!* No one had expected the campaign ahead would center on this everyday substance. Yes, it was one of the eleven demands Gandhi had presented to Irwin, but to make it the keystone of their independence struggle was something else altogether. Could this possibly be the "fight of such magnitude" Gandhi had been promising over the past several days?

Salt?! How could this rally the nation, far and wide? Salt?! Compared to the taxes on liquor or cloth, salt represented a pittance of tax revenue for the British. Would people march in the streets, sacrifice themselves in the face of violent opposition, for this? Salt?! Several in the room pushed back against the idea. "Do you expect us all to go out and just make salt?"

Naidu was used to being surprised by Gandhi. Born into a family of Brahmins, the highest caste in India, Naidu was a child prodigy who had enrolled in the University of Madras at the age of twelve. Afterward, at sixteen, she studied at King's College in London, then at Cambridge. Her early poetry had won the respect of everybody from Oscar Wilde to Henry James. While in England, Naidu fell in love with a young medical student of a lower caste, and against her parents' wishes, she married him. They returned to India and had four children in five years.

Naidu's first book of poetry, published in 1905, made her famous. Her second followed in 1912, to similar success. Although she wrote her poems in English first, they spoke, as one biographer noted, "to the young wives and mothers of India [and Naidu] became the voice of all women in her land." This brought her into the women's suffragist movement in India, then the freedom struggle against the Raj.

The day she and Gandhi met, on the eve of World War I, she had tracked him down while he was visiting London. She found him on the top floor of a decrepit house, sitting cross-legged on a dirty black carpet, eating what looked like a beggar's meal out of a wooden bowl. Naidu was amazed that this curious little man with his shaved head was the one who had made such great strides for Indian rights in South Africa. Over the years, however, she had come to trust Gandhi's instincts. Still, she could not quite believe this was his "great decision." Jawaharlal Nehru was stunned too. Salt?! Only his father, Motilal Nehru, the aging nationalist, saw the brilliance in it. He curtly told his son, "The only wonder is no one else thought of it."

Salt! Ancient civilizations across the world thought salt a "divine substance." Without salt and water, the human body cannot nourish or sustain itself. A typical adult contains 250 grams of salt—roughly four saltshakers—but is persistently losing it through sweat and other bodily processes. Journalist Mark Kurlansky, who wrote an entire book about salt, remarked that salt "fills the ocean, bubbles up from springs, forms crusts in lake beds, and thickly veins a large part of the earth's rock . . . Salt is so common, so easy to obtain, and so inexpensive that we have forgotten that from the beginning of civilization . . . [it] was one of the most sought-after commodities in human history."

Trade routes and whole cities were formed because of salt. The first great Roman road was named Via Salaria, the Salt Road. Wars and revolutions and pirating adventures were fought for it.

Salt ships traveled in convoys to forestall attack. And throughout history, from ancient governments to modern ones, salt was monopolized and taxed. The Han dynasty in China expanded its empire on the back of salt revenues. After all, everyone needed salt to live, and it had myriad other uses, from preserving food, to producing gunpowder, making medicines, and even, at times, serving as currency.

As the Congress members at the ashram that morning knew, India boasted an abundance of salt. For thousands of years, it had been mined in the Punjab and could be easily harvested from natural salt beds across India's vast coastlines. When the British came, they made it illegal to harvest salt without paying the Raj a salt tax. And with the Indian Salt Act of 1882, they protected their control of salt and raised their taxes on it. According to the law, salt could be collected and manufactured only at specific government-sanctioned depots. It could not be sold without a license or exported outside India. Any violation of the law was punishable by fines and imprisonment.

Gandhi's reasoning was that he could have selected other British tariffs and taxes—textiles, land, sugar, tea—but nothing showed more starkly the injustice of the Raj than the tax on salt. Indians could scoop up with their bare hands this necessity of life all along the thousands of miles of their own country's shorelines, and yet they were forbidden from doing so without first paying their foreign masters. Gandhi's own mentor, the renowned Indian social reformer Gopal Krishna Gokhale, had railed against the salt tax as early as 1902. He said it caused "unquestioned hardship [on] the poorest of the poor of our community."

By the end of the meeting, Gandhi had made his case. He was still finalizing the exact form the civil disobedience campaign would take, but he determined to make a start with only those followers whose discipline and faith in nonviolence he considered guaranteed: his Satyagraha ashramites. Fearing that his female ashramites might be molested and defiled by government troops in any campaign, he decided that only his male ashramites should be involved. That would exclude Naidu, neither an ashram resident nor a man, even though she wished she could join the campaign immediately. Before going to bed that night, she wrote to her daughter, "No one seems particularly enthusiastic, and everyone is more than a little doubtful how things will pan out. (That sounds like a pun on salt!) The Little Man is chockful of cheek and conceit and he will need all of it and more to take him even halfway."

Chapter 4

Lord Irwin deliberately neglected to personally welcome Gandhi's messenger when he arrived at Viceroy's House on March 4, 1930. There was no doubt about when Reginald Reynolds was due. Over the previous two days, the newspapers, including the conservative *Times of India*, reported his imminent arrival. Reynolds was an English Quaker, aged twenty-four. He had been living at Gandhi's ashram and clearly, Irwin thought, he had come under the spell of the nationalist leader and had lost his way. Meeting Gandhi would be a mistake. Irwin instructed his private secretary, George Cunningham, to receive Reynolds instead and to accept from him the letter from Gandhi that he had brought with him. The contents of the letter were no less striking to Irwin than Cunningham's description of the messenger who had delivered it. Reynolds had been wearing coarsely spun khadi and sandals—much in the style of Gandhi himself.

"Dear friend," the letter opened. "Before embarking on civil disobedience and taking a risk I have dreaded to take all these years, I would fain approach you and find a way out."

Gandhi went on to call British rule "a curse" that had impoverished his nation, demeaned its culture, and reduced his people to little more than serfs. If these evils, among others, were not made right, then, Gandhi said, he had no choice but to launch a nonviolent campaign against the salt laws. "As the independence movement is essentially for the poorest in the land, a beginning will be made with this evil. The wonder is we have submitted to the cruel monopoly for so long." Gandhi concluded his letter by saying that his demands were not a threat but a "a simple and sacred duty" and signed it, "I remain your sincere friend. M. K. Gandhi."

Irwin was left bewildered over what to do. There he was, the representative of the British Crown in India, essentially the autocrat of 320 million souls, and one of his subjects, addressing him like an Oxford college mate, had just laid down the gauntlet. It had been gently placed, not thrown, but it was, nonetheless, a gauntlet.

Irwin believed in the righteous nature of British imperialism. He believed it uplifted its subjects, strengthened his own country, and acted as a promoter of world peace. Unlike some of his peers back in London, he was far from an imperialist zealot who thought the "natives" would either never be ready for their own self-government or would be ready only hundreds of years in the future. Irwin considered self-government inevitable in the much nearer term and thought that it was his job to gradually pave the way. In this respect, he was an outlier in the Conservative Party, and a new kind of viceroy.

After his arrival in India, in March 1926, Irwin spent his first couple of years focused mostly on calming the age-old strife between the Hindu and Muslim communities, a move that ran against the long-standing British tradition of furthering their divide. His pleas of "all-India patriotism" fell mostly on deaf ears, however, and deadly riots between the two communities grew. Meanwhile, the independence movement was a sputtering affair of little threat. Gandhi had kept largely out of politics after his release from prison in 1924. The Indian National Congress was well numbered, but it was more a middle-class Hindu party than a populist one that represented the diversity of the whole country. There were also many moderates who wanted to maintain close relations with Britain.

Then came Parliament's formation of the Simon Commission, sparking renewed demands for self-government. Terrorist acts were on the upswing. Young leaders like Jawaharlal Nehru were calling for the "complete severance of association with Britain." And now, Gandhi had returned once more to the center of affairs, threatening an immediate campaign against the Raj to bring about independence.

Irwin was pelted with advice. Sir Frederick Sykes, the governor of Bombay, cabled to tell him it was critical that any resistance against the salt laws be stopped with "firm action at the outset of the movement, giving a clear lead and assurance to the loyal population." Charles Innes, the governor of another British colony, Burma, agreed: "Strike hard and quick at the leaders." Correspondence from London was equally firm. On first hearing of this letter from Gandhi, Winston Churchill urged toughness. Although his Conservative Party was recently out of power—he had served as chancellor of the exchequer in its government—the fifty-six-year-old politician was an ardent imperialist and never one to hold his tongue, particularly since the Crown was losing control of Ireland and Egypt. "Upon the supreme issue of India, the British Empire will arise in its old strength," Churchill said.

London newspapers, reflecting the feelings of Parliament, chimed in as well. The *Daily Mail*'s publisher thundered, "We're not going to allow the fate of [India] to be ruined by the folly of a handful of excited nationalists." The *Daily Telegraph* predicted the salt campaign would likely "turn out to be a very small and cowardly mouse."

During numerous meetings in the halls of Viceroy's House, walks in the gardens, even alone in his wood-paneled study, his dogs asleep at his feet, Irwin wavered between action and patience.

Soon after receiving Gandhi's ultimatum, he wrote to his father, Viscount Halifax. "We have begun to have our troublesome time, but I feel pretty certain that it is right to jump on Gandhi and the other leaders as soon as they do anything illegal, and though this will make a great row, I think it would make as big a row later when the conditions might probably be worse."

Irwin's staff prepared a report that noted, "Salt does not appear, at first, to be a very promising field in which to inaugurate a campaign . . . The most that would happen would be that relatively small quantities of bad salt would be sporadically produced." Weighing this analysis and his own instincts, Irwin decided not to open independence talks with Gandhi. His whole threat against the salt tax might fizzle into nothing. Irwin decided to allow events to play themselves out a little further—though if anyone flagrantly violated the law, he would have them arrested.

Irwin let two days go by before composing a reply to Gandhi, and though the viceroy had a hand in its composition, he had his private secretary, Cunningham, deliver the response. It was curtly worded; there was no need for threats or point-by-point rebuttals to Gandhi's arguments. "His Excellency, the viceroy, desires me to acknowledge your letter . . . He regrets to learn that you contemplate a course of action which is clearly bound to involve violation of the law and danger to the public peace."

In the three weeks after announcing the nonviolent resistance campaign, Gandhi delivered broadsides against the salt tax in speeches, newspaper interviews, and his own writings. He wanted national—and international—publicity for the campaign. "Next to air and water," he declared in one widely quoted article, "salt is perhaps the greatest necessity of life . . . The tax constitutes the most inhuman poll tax that ingenuity of man can devise." He added, "The illegality is in a government that steals the people's salt and makes them pay heavily for the stolen article. The people, when they become conscious of their power, will have every right to take possession of what belongs to them."

While drumming up attention to the salt tax, Gandhi also prepared those at the ashram who would serve as the vanguard of the campaign against it. First, he tightened the rules, including those about strict punctuality at prayer meetings, khadi-spinning quotas, and daily diary-keeping. Discipline, even in the small things, would be of utmost importance once they became satyagraha warriors.

Second, he posted a list of commandments, beginning with a clear explanation of his nonviolent manifesto. "Satyagraha literally means insistence on truth . . . There is in it no room for violence. The only force of universal application can, therefore, be that of ahimsa or love. In other words, it is soul force. It follows, therefore, that a civil resister, while he will strain every nerve to compass the end of the existing rule, will do no intentional injury in thought, word, or deed to a single Englishman." Among the commandments were: to harbor no anger but to suffer it; to endure assaults but never to retaliate; to voluntarily submit to arrest but never to any order delivered in anger, even if one feared violence or punishment; to never insult one's opponent.

But how exactly would they fight the salt tax, many asked. Gandhi stalled revealing the answer. He had come to it himself only a few days after the Congress meeting in mid-February, and he was still considering whether indeed it was the right way to proceed. Unlike the decision to focus on salt, which came gradually to him, the method of rebellion came in a flash of inspiration.

A march.

If Lord Irwin did not accept the demands of his letter, Gandhi would stage a march that would culminate in the collecting of salt at the seashore, overtly breaking the law. Along the way, he would rally support for the movement so that once his band of satyagrahis violated the salt laws in that area, a tide of millions would do the same in villages and cities across India.

Gandhi had experience with such marches. In 1913, in South Africa, he had led almost 2,300 Indian settlers, including whole families, on a five-day journey from the province of Natal over the border into neighboring Transvaal. British Empire officials had made this kind of border-crossing illegal without a permit, and Gandhi violated the restriction to protest racist and oppressive legislation against the Indian community. Early in the march, the South African government arrested Gandhi, leaving his followers to carry on without him. Nonetheless, the march drew much attention, and in time, the movement improved the rights of his fellow Indians.

Gandhi did not want to mimic the Transvaal march, however. The large, unwieldy group had often felt out of control; the campaign had lasted only a few days; and the area they passed through was rife with white South Africans who threatened to "shoot the Indians like rabbits." This time, he wanted a tight, disciplined group of marchers, all the better to ensure the maintenance of nonviolence. A journey much longer than five days would give them more time to raise awareness of their cause. And he wanted to travel through countryside where they would have support of the people in whose name they were fighting. The obvious place to start was the rural countryside around Ahmedabad. First, this was where Gandhi lived, and he held a lot of support. Second, the nearby Gujarati coastline stretched 992 miles and was rich with deposits of salt.

In 1928, under Gandhi's guidance, his close associate Vallabhbhai Patel had led a civil disobedience campaign in the township of Bardoli in southern Gujarat against a sizable increase in land taxes. As a local of the area and with the peasants already suffering from a famine, Patel won quick backing among the population, and ultimately, the Bombay Presidency (the administrative subdivision of the Raj that controlled the vast Gujarat area) backed down on the taxes. Gandhi considered the Bardoli Satyagraha proof that India was ready for his methods on a much bigger scale.

On March 5, 1930, the day after Reynolds delivered the letter to the viceroy, Gandhi revealed to his followers the nature of their campaign against the salt laws. After evening prayers, he explained that the campaign would begin the following week. There would be fifty marchers, and they would leave directly from the ashram. Vallabhbhai Patel departed immediately to fire up the locals in the area, defying the authorities who had forbidden him from speaking publicly after his success in Bardoli. In one impassioned address at an outdoor meeting in Broach, he promised a "war unprecedented in the history of the world would commence soon."

The following evening, Gandhi received the terse response from Lord Irwin's private secretary, and then came the news that Patel had been arrested and imprisoned by a district magistrate for addressing a public meeting in another village. "On bended knees I asked for bread," Gandhi announced. "And I have received stone instead."

The march would now move forward.

As news of the march spread, letters and telegrams streamed into the ashram, notably from university students throughout India. "[May I offer] my humble services as a satyagrahi in the coming struggle," wrote one student. "We are determined to join your campaign, but we are disallowed by our parents," wrote another. They would have to exercise patience, Gandhi replied. He would only allow marchers who "had gone through the rigid discipline of the ashram, who tried to follow truth and nonviolence in thought, word, and deed."

The majority of Gandhi's ashramites volunteered to join. He interviewed each one to determine whether they were indeed prepared for the sacrifices that lay ahead. He selected a range of individuals. Young and old. High caste and low. Hindus, Christians, Muslims, and Sikhs. Musicians, poets, farmers, mechanics, lawyers, and soldiers. Some were Untouchables who had never had more than a few rupees in their pockets, and others had been born with silver spoons in their mouths. One was the reformed disciple of an Indian terrorist organization now dedicated to peaceful methods. This was the small army that would dare face down the power and might of the British Empire.

Notably absent from Gandhi's selection of fifty were women—despite angered pleas and letters from numerous ashram women as well as Sarojini Naidu. Gandhi promised they would have a role after the march ended but not on the journey itself. "I must be considerate to the opponent," he justified. "We want to go in for suffering, and there may even be torture."

Over the next few days, the roster grew from fifty to seventy-nine, including Gandhi himself. So too did the distance of the march. He initially thought it would be roughly thirty to forty miles from the ashram to an area where there were inland salt deposits. Then he changed his mind and decided to go to the seashore at Dandi, a small village to the south, where they would break the law by the mere act of picking up salt left by the retreating tides. Volunteers from the local university were sent to scout out the route. The journey would take twenty-four days and cover roughly 220 miles.

Doubters questioned Gandhi's course of action. A Gujarati politician asked, "Wouldn't the Salt Campaign fail to arouse the enthusiasm of the youth of the nation? Wouldn't they all see through the farce of wielding the sledgehammer of satyagraha to kill the fly of the Salt Act?" Others called the march a "damp squib" or a "kindergarten stage of revolution" that would spur few to action. An editorial in *The New Statesman*, a British magazine, remarked, "It is difficult not to laugh, and we imagine that will be the mood of most thinking Indians. There is something almost childishly theatrical in challenging in this way the salt monopoly."

Motilal Nehru, who had liked the idea of the Salt March at first, now worried that salt had become yet another "hobby horse," like spinning, and would result in a whole lot of nothing. Even Gandhi's long-standing personal secretary, Mahadev Desai, begged him to change his program and to concentrate on something else.

His mind now set, Gandhi stood firm.

As he dearly wanted, Manilal Gandhi was invited to join the column of marchers. He had never considered his inclusion a given, and to be chosen for the great campaign ahead, to be at his father's side, brought him immense pride. It was not easy to be the son of the Mahatma, a living saint, and his father had always set a higher standard and asked more of his own four sons than any of his other followers. Manilal's efforts in South Africa running the *Indian Opinion* had rarely been good enough for his father, and his criticism had been sharp and persistent.

Now, on March 11, 1930, the eve of their departure, Manilal prepared his kit. In two cloth satchels he packed a change of clothes, his bedding roll, his diary and pencil, a small wooden charka, a worn edition of the Bhagavad Gita, and a mug. All the marchers were to wear a uniform: khadi trousers, a shawl, and a simple white khadi cap. They would not wear badges or any other insignia, and they would not carry flags. He did not need to bring food or water. These would be provided by the villages along their route, arranged by the same advance party of university students who had already left for the first village stop along the way.

That afternoon, Gandhi delivered a calm but impactful talk to the marchers. "Either we shall win the goal for which we are marching or die in the attempt to win it . . . We will keep on our fight till swaraj is established in India. This will be the last fight." He then told those like Manilal, who had wives and children, that they should be clear about the sacrifice ahead. There would be "no retreat" for "the first soldiers of the country's freedom battle." He offered them one last chance to pull out. No one took him up on it.

Still, Manilal and the others feared what was to come. Gandhi might be arrested before they even had a chance to leave. The police were rumored to already be on their way to the ashram. Troops were reported to be coming to stop the march. Some among them believed they would be killed before they even left the outskirts of Ahmedabad. Scaremongering scuttlebutt had the British bombing them from the air or tearing their ranks apart from a machine gun nest on a bridge.

Whatever lay ahead, the eyes of the world were now on them. For the past few days, reporters, photographers, and newsreel crews had been moving into the area. They crowded the gates of the ashram, and Manilal often found his father being interviewed, answering reporters' questions while sitting cross-legged facing them.

If you are arrested, what will happen? "The fight should continue," Gandhi replied. Congress and Nehru would take the lead. *What if the march leads to violence?* There is more likely to be violence, Gandhi said, if there was no "safety-valve in the shape of a movement of nonviolence."

The press was far outnumbered by the swelling crowds converging on the ashram. People crossed the shallow waters of the river by foot to reach the grounds of the settlement. They arrived by motorcar, by horse-drawn carriage, and by bullock cart, stirring up a wake of dust that obscured the miles of traffic snarling the road. By 7:00 p.m., when Gandhi prepared to speak to the gathering crowd of supporters, there were over ten thousand people crammed onto the sandy shores of the river—the only space big enough to accommodate them. People craned their necks and pressed forward to get a glimpse of the Mahatma. Manilal and several ashramites made a circle around him and locked arms to prevent a surge from overwhelming him.

Bold of tone, Gandhi began: "In all probability this will be my last speech to you. Even if the government allows me to march tomorrow morning, this will be my last speech on the sacred banks of the Sabarmati. Possibly these may be the last words of my life here." He then explained exactly how they should exercise civil disobedience from the moment he was arrested: breaking the salt laws wherever they could, manufacturing salt, selling it, picking it up freely from the shore. For every group of satyagrahis thrown into prison—or worse—ten more should stand in their place. He concluded, "A satyagrahi, whether free or incarcerated, is ever victorious. He is vanquished only when he forsakes truth and nonviolence . . . God bless you all and keep off all obstacles from the path in the struggle that begins tomorrow."

That night, Gandhi kept to his quarters—certain of his impending arrest. Kasturba, ever the pillar supporting her husband, rubbed oil on his head to soothe him as he wrote his letters. The crowds outside the ashram gates continued to shout slogans and sing. One of their favorites was the "Vande Mataram," a famous Bengali poem praising the motherland of India. Whenever there was noise from an engine, the crowd grew immediately silent, expecting the arrival of the police. Sleep did not come easily for Manilal. This could well be his last night with his family. The sacrifice Gandhi spoke of was not empty words. In joining the march, Manilal had committed to this fight, and there was every possibility it might mean his death.

Chapter 5

Despite everyone's fears, the police did not come in the night to arrest Gandhi. At 4:00 a.m., the dull clang of a bell sounded throughout the ashram, and, one by one, the Dandi marchers awakened—those who had managed at least a few hours of sleep. On the road outside the ashram gates, the crowds remained. They huddled around small fires in the chilly morning and sang Hindu songs in the hours before dawn.

Kasturba Gandhi had been up long before the prayer bell rang. At the ashram, she was affectionately referred to as Ba or "Great Mother"—all the marchers were her children in a way. She prepared breakfast as well as a meal of flatbread and boiled vegetables for the marchers to carry with them on the road. Among them was Anand Hingorani. A twenty-four-year-old graduate of the University of Bombay, he had joined the ashram after the Lahore session of Congress. He showed up at the gates in a suit, tie, and hat and tried to tip one of the inhabitants who helped him with his two trunks of belongings. He had quickly taken to the life.

So too had Ratnaji, who was born into a family of Untouchables from Gujarat. Gandhi referred to Untouchables (a colonial term) as harijan, "Children of God." For over three millennia, Hindus divided their society into four main groups determined by birth, from the highest, the Brahmans, who were typically priests, teachers, and intellectuals, to the lowest, the Shudras, who did menial jobs. Each of these groups, or castes, had countless subgroups. Untouchables existed outside the caste system, such was their even lowlier standing. They were not even perceived as part of Hindu society. This was the basis for their being given the worst jobs, enduring slave-like exploitation, and suffering public humiliation. They were forbidden from drinking from the same wells or attending the same temples as others. For many years, Gandhi had labored to end the terrible discrimination they suffered. In 1922, Ratnaji, a weaver by trade, had entered the ashram to marry a girl whose family already lived there. Three other harijans would also be marching.

Two Muslims had been selected. One was Abbasbhai. A teacher and the ashram's barber, he was also responsible for waking everybody for first prayers. Some months before, Abbasbhai had overslept by ten minutes. Gandhi had upbraided him for wasting ten minutes not only of his time but that amount multiplied by the hundreds of ashramites. Abbasbhai had learned the lesson, which was one of the reasons why Gandhi wanted him on the march.

Age did not matter. One of the marchers was only sixteen years old; another was over sixty. Commitment was everything, and once they enlisted, there was no hiding. Their names, ages, birthplaces, and professions had been published two days earlier by Gandhi as the "first batch of Satyagrahis."

Kasturba understood this commitment better than most. Her husband, her son Manilal, and her nineteen-year-old grandson, Kantilal, were all leaving that morning. As worried as she was about the dangers that lay ahead for them, it was her duty to help as best she could. Kasturba bent her life to align with her husband's pursuits, as she had done over their many decades together.

She was from a well-to-do merchant family, but, as was usual at the time, her education had focused on her becoming a good mother and wife rather than on academic subjects. Kasturba's and Mohandas's families had long been friends in Porbandar, the small port city on the Arabian Sea where the two grew up and were married as teenagers in an arranged marriage. In the first years of their marriage, Mohandas was a somewhat shy boy, uncertain of his future and abilities. Never in her wildest imagination did Kasturba see in him the makings of a mahatma. Enduring a life of voluntary poverty, giving up jewelry and nice clothes, eating a bland diet, living with Untouchables, suffering threats of violence, raising children without a traditional education, abstaining from sex with her husband—none of this came easily for Kasturba. There were fights, and there was bitterness, but they always stayed together.

Kasturba may have been in her extraordinary husband's shadow, but she was a leader in her own right too. In South Africa, she helped start their first communal settlement. She marched and suffered arrest, same as her husband. On their return to India, she was rarely absent from his campaigns, and she was a grounding influence at the ashram. That morning, she was present when her husband gave a brief talk to the marchers on the prayer grounds, saying, "We are entering upon a life-and-death struggle," and she was present again when Gandhi emerged from his room, accompanied by one of the viceroy's emissaries who was trying to broker a last-minute deal to stop the campaign. No doubt, Kasturba knew it was a fruitless attempt. Her husband's words still hung in her mind as the sun rose.

As 6:30 a.m. and the march's start approached, Gandhi took his position at the front of the column of marchers who had assembled in front of the gate. Always conscious of time and schedules, he wore a large watch pinned to the khadi draped across his shoulders and carried a long, iron-tipped bamboo staff to steady his stride along the many miles ahead. The seventy-eight marchers behind him stood two in a row.

Although the bustle and noise from the crowd assembled outside continued, inside the ashram felt like a quiet universe of its own. Kasturba watched as her daughter-in-law, Sushila, said goodbye to Manilal. Tears poured down the twenty-two-year-old's face, and her whole body trembled. Finally she tore herself loose, ran back to Kasturba, and buried her head in her mother-in-law's shoulder. Kasturba noticed many of the other wives and mothers crying as well. Gently, she pulled up Sushila and said, "Do you want your husband to carry with him the image of a weeping wife? . . . Our men are warriors. We are warriors' wives. We must give the men courage. If we are brave, they will be brave."

With that, Kasturba walked along the line of marchers until she reached Mohandas. Everything that needed to be said was shared in the meeting of their eyes. Kasturba placed a garland of khadi around his neck and pressed her finger into a mixture she had made of ghee and vermilion powder, which she carried on a brass plate, and daubed a red tilak dot on her husband's forehead. The mark, according to Hindu scriptures, was meant "to protect and purify the mind as well as the body." In her view, as her grandson later wrote, "It was an invocation of good fortune for the departing traveler, and a prayer for his safe return." She then offered to daub a dot on the forehead of each marcher as he passed. Sushila would never forget the look on Kasturba's face. It was one of "fearless determination" that steeled every individual in the column, including Manilal and Kantilal.

At last, the Satyagraha Ashram gates opened. A musician strummed an ektara, a traditional instrument with one string, and the marchers sang a Gandhi favorite, "Vaishnava Jana To." The fifteenth-century devotional hymn about self-sacrifice started, "One who is a Vaishnava [a Hindu sect], knows the pain of others, does good to others, without letting pride enter his mind." Kasturba watched her husband lead the way as the marchers headed out onto the road. Only after they had all filed out would she follow and join them for the first part of the journey.

A wide grin on his face, Gandhi walked southward from the

ashram, his strides quickly eating up the ground. Those behind hurried to keep up. *So much for the slow old man*, many must have thought. Before long, the swell of the crowds along both sides of the road slowed his pace. "Men and women, boys and girls, millionaires and mill-workers had come to see the beginning of Gandhi's march," wrote one reporter. Lining the road as far as the

eye could see, they waved flags and shouted well-wishes. Some of the marchers took a moment outside the gates of the ashram to receive blessings from a group of young girls who pressed grains of rice into the red dots on their foreheads. A band started playing "God Save the King" before suddenly registering that it was inappropriate for the occasion and stopping midway.

As the marchers continued along the route, some people threw flowers at their feet. Others tossed rupee notes, donations to the cause. Coconuts were cracked open—a symbolic act of offering oneself to God—in the belief that this would bring good fortune. There was a spirit of celebration and joyfulness. The sheer number of people around the ashram—twenty thousand, perhaps more—almost overwhelmed Gandhi's column. One marcher wrote, "The route for seven miles resembled a sea of humanity through which we had to wade. You could at no time see the beginning of the procession—you might say it was a beginningless, unending procession." Mammoth clouds of dust kicked up by the crowds stung people's eyes and choked the air.

Onward, Gandhi walked, following the river into the city. At that point, Kasturba and a longtime friend, Abbas Tyabji, moved alongside him. If Gandhi was arrested, he intended Tyabji to take over as leader of the salt campaign. At seventy-six years of age, Tyabji was an old lion of the resistance, but he had come to it late in his life. Born into a prominent Gujarati family (his uncle had been the first Indian judge on the Bombay High Court), Abbas had studied law in London, much as Gandhi had done. Tyabji became a chief judge, and although a moderate nationalist, he had remained loyal to the Raj until the Jallianwala Bagh massacre. Appointed by the Indian National Congress as chair of a fact-finding commission to investigate what had happened, he quickly became horrified at the atrocities, resigned his judgeship, and joined with Gandhi in the freedom struggle. Before that time, recalled Tyabji's daughter,

Raihana, their family was aristocratic and anglicized. Afterward, "All our clothes, the richest clothes, silks, velvets, satins, gold, silver, all were burnt . . . We had committed ourselves to khadi."

Gandhi headed into Ahmedabad, his staff striking the road with the rhythm of a metronome. Spectators who had failed to gain a place on the streets climbed atop roofs, terraces, walls, and even trees to watch the procession go by. When they spotted Gandhi, they shouted, "Gandhi ki jai!" ("Victory to Gandhi!") Indeed, it seemed like the whole world was watching. The herd of reporters and cameramen shoving their way to the front of the crowds made sure of that.

All kinds of grand words were spoken about the march's first moments. In a newspaper editorial, P. C. Ray, an Indian nationalist and renowned chemistry professor, compared it to "the exodus of Israelites under Moses." "Like the historic march of Ramachandra to Lanka," observed Motilal Nehru at the time. "Today the pilgrim marches onward on his long trek," added his son Jawaharlal.

Despite the festive air of these comments, Gandhi understood that the road ahead promised to be long. He was surprised that the viceroy had yet to order his arrest but knew that this could happen at any moment. Until then, he would set the pace. He had been glad to see the tremendous crowds—surpassing seventy thousand in total—throughout the city. He found their presence a good omen. But if they were just gawkers and did nothing to support the cause, they were adding little value. When the time came, he needed all the people of India to take action.

Gandhi led his column of marchers toward the arched steel structure of the Ellis Bridge that spanned the Sabarmati River. The bridge itself was packed with masses of people, but once the marchers were past it, the numbers along the roadside dwindled. The marchers themselves crossed the river along a shallow riverbed south of the bridge. On the opposite shore, Gandhi wrapped his arm around Kasturba and said his goodbyes.

The two were used to farewells.

Followed now by children on bicycles, the column moved down another dusty road. An occasional truck idled alongside, with a newspaper photographer standing in the truck bed, trying to catch a shot of Gandhi. The marchers took a brief rest at Chandola Lake, a thumbprint of murky water southeast of the city. By this point the crowd numbered only a few thousand, and Gandhi made a brief speech to those who remained, calling on them to "go back and resolve to do your share."

The police remained surprisingly absent.

When the marchers departed from the lake, a feeling of calm settled over the column. The roadside was largely free of bystanders, the air cleared of dust as a result, and they could at last see the open stretch of fields that lay ahead. Four hours—and thirteen miles—into their march, they stopped at Aslali village. They were welcomed by turbaned dancers, a band of musicians, and a path strewn with flowers. The late-morning sun was hot, and they took shade under a pair of enormous mango trees. The vanguard of students had arranged for meals to be ready when they arrived. As one marcher wrote in his diary of March 12, "It was a perfect end of a perfect day."

They could not return home until they had won swaraj, Gandhi told the assembly of villagers: "The soldiers of the first batch had burned their boats the moment the march began." Over the next several hours, he gave more speeches, wrote several letters, spun khadi yarn, and gave interviews to several journalists. His work kept him up until well past midnight when the dark canopy of the sky glittered with stars. Gandhi was tired. He had not walked that far in years. It was a good tired, though—well earned.

They would stay in Aslali until early the next morning, the first leg of their long march complete.

Chapter 6

The next morning, March 13, just as the sky was beginning to lighten on the horizon, the marchers filed out of Aslali. The day before, with its gargantuan crowds and bustling excitement, Manilal Gandhi had felt thankful to be playing a part in this important movement. He could be excused for not sustaining that sentiment into the second day. Few of the villagers were awake to join the marchers in their morning prayers or to bid them farewell after their spare meal of warm porridge and bread. The garlands of flowers and the rousing cheers of the day before were but a memory.

The marchers walked quietly out of town in the half dark, followed only by a pair of oxcarts. Alone on the road, bordered on either side by long expanses of green paddy fields, they advanced toward Bareja, a village six miles away, where they would stop before the morning heat became overwhelming. Manilal found the going easy, though parts of the road were so thick with dust it coated his legs.

Others were not doing so well. His father had made it clear before they departed that those who could not maintain the pace would have to return to the ashram. Several already had such terrible blisters on their feet that they tried to go barefoot on the road, only to find that the soles of their feet were cut and bruised by the loose stones. One marcher had to sit atop the oxcart carrying their charkas. Another was growing weaker by the step. He had been running a fever ever since he woke up, and as much as he attempted to hide how he felt, it was clear he was quite sick.

Manilal knew that his father was struggling too. At the ashram, nobody had openly questioned whether Gandhi would be able to sustain a twenty-four-day march in the deadly heat. Already, on only their second day, he seemed to be faltering. His pace was sluggish, and he had to rest his arms on the shoulders of two teenage marchers. A brief conversation with him revealed that not only did he too have blisters, but, worse, he was also suffering a flare-up of his rheumatism. Each step he took sent pain lancing through his joints. "It is of no consequence," Gandhi stated bluntly. "I must reach Dandi on the day decided upon, whatever happens." Manilal and the others would have gladly carried him for a spell, but he refused, and he refused the offer of riding in the oxcart as well.

After two and a half hours of walking, much of it on roads cutting through rice fields, the marchers reached Bareja. Only a scattering of people came out to welcome them, and there was no fanfare. The village headman wished them success, but he did not resign from his post (an administrative role established by the British), as

Gandhi hoped he would, and as he hoped would happen in each town along their route. Without local leaders to collect taxes and enforce the viceroy's mandates, the Raj would have no real power over the people. The report on Bareja that had been drawn up by the advance party of university students troubled Gandhi too. The schools were shabby, and the upper castes abused the Untouchables, contrary to Gandhi's teachings.

The marchers made their way to their resting spot. They passed a filthy pond and open latrines. Since returning to India from South Africa, Gandhi had made it one of his missions to improve the sanitation and cleanliness of villages, and the Bareja villagers were clearly not making any efforts on that front. Further, nobody was wearing khadi, another sign that Gandhi's teachings on self-sufficiency were not followed there. A mere few hundred people, from a village of 2,500 inhabitants, gathered to hear Gandhi speak. Even though the platform from which he spoke was covered by a square of khadi stretched between four poles, the shade barely softened the unbearable heat of the sun. Manilal could hear the pain in his father's voice as he encouraged those gathered to wear khadi instead of British-spun cloth. Then he spoke of the sad state of their village. "If we cannot put our own house in order in an organized manner, then how shall we run the country's government?"

After the huge outpouring of support in Ahmedabad and in Aslali, one had to wonder whether enthusiasm for the Salt March had already peaked, and that they might now have nothing but the drudgery of a long, blistering walk ahead. It was easy to fear that if support dwindled in the villages, the entire campaign would sputter into nothing—whether they reached Dandi or not.

On Saturday, March 15, Lord Irwin was in his study at Viceroy's House, leafing through a pile of newspaper articles and official reports about Gandhi and his march. Only his dogs, sleeping at his feet, seemed not to have an opinion on recent events.

"The historic march for freedom was celebrated by the people of Gujarat," remarked the pro-nationalist *Bombay Chronicle*. According to its reporter, Gandhi and his marchers had been met at the village of Matar, and at their next stop, by a welcoming committee, a sizable purse of donations, and the resignation of several village officials. Another newspaper detailed that a phalanx of ten thousand satyagrahis were at the ready to come to the campaign's aid—or to "fill the jails of the country"—when Gandhi called on them. Still another newspaper had even consulted an astrologer to predict the fate of the march. According to the seer, the planets were aligned in a "happy" confluence that guaranteed victory for Gandhi; as for the British government, they would "assume a compromising attitude."

To many observers throughout India, particularly on the first morning of the march, the rise of a mass civil disobedience movement seemed certain. In Bombay, Calcutta, and towns big and small, thousands came out to support the end of the salt tax. On that first day too, from his family home in Allahabad, Jawaharlal Nehru issued a proclamation through the nationalist press for all of India to ready themselves. This included enrolling and training volunteers, selecting areas in which to break the salt laws, and spreading the word about the developing movement. "Each hour is important and cannot be wasted," Nehru said. Once the government stopped the marchers—or arrested Gandhi—then the nationwide campaign would really begin.

Nehru's threats did not stir Irwin to take action. He was deliberately holding back from any crackdown, not wanting to add any fuel to the salt campaign. He knew that the next few days might still prove that Gandhi's march was a whole lot of fuss about nothing. Pro-British newspapers pushed that viewpoint. They called the march a sad, "theatrical" spectacle. "Evidently, there is no popular feeling behind the movement," one said dismissively. "The scenes would have been amusing if they had not been pathetic."

Reports from Irwin's own officials in Gujarat mirrored these descriptions. Gandhi may have attracted "deep veneration" in Ahmedabad, but afterward the crowds were "orderly" and "not so large." The Muslim community was not behind the movement, and the "poor reception" in Bareja was evidence that the marchers' welcome was at best dependent on who was in charge of each village. Finally, they reported, Gandhi appeared to be in failing health already—as were several other marchers.

As to what the viceroy should do now, everybody seemed to have an opinion on that too. Many in the British Parliament continued to rail against Irwin for not responding more harshly after receiving the initial letter from Gandhi. They felt that Gandhi was risking a repeat of the violence that had occurred at Chauri Chaura. To prevent such a thing from happening, British conservatives called for an immediate show of force. This view was advanced most stridently by Sir Michael O'Dwyer, who had been lieutenant governor of the Punjab at the time of the Jallianwala Bagh massacre. In a widely published editorial, O'Dwyer argued, "If you look round India today you see that the spirit of rebellion, which in 1919 we crushed promptly and drastically—and that in the long run is the most humane course—is again abroad."

Others preached moderation, believing that Irwin was right not to arrest Gandhi. Doing so would only draw sympathy to Gandhi's campaign and incite the Indian people to further action. The governor of Assam, Sir Egbert Laurie Hammond, simply joked, "The best thing to do with Gandhi is to allow him to manufacture salt and then confiscate and tell him to increase his output."

Irwin was capable of making up his own mind. In a public speech early in his viceroyship, he announced that he had a "double duty." First, he was "under the plain obligation of seeing that the king's government in India is carried on, with due respect for the law." Second, but no less critical, he must "endeavor to interpret as faithfully as he may the hopes, the feelings, the desires of the Indian people" to Great Britain.

On his arrival in Bombay, almost four years before, he had made clear that he was a different kind of viceroy. Yes, there had been the typical lavish welcome ceremonies heralding his arrival, but he had also begged off for three hours to attend Good Friday services at an Anglican cathedral. Irwin's deep faith in God impressed many within India.

It is true that Irwin availed himself of the many perks of being viceroy, just as those who had gone before him had done. Winters in the plains of Delhi. Summers in the high hills of Simla. Christmas in Calcutta. He participated in the tiger hunts, safaris, horse races, polo tournaments, gala dinners, and sumptuous balls. He spent weekends as a guest at the palaces of the maharajas—the princes who had once ruled India and who the British allowed to retain some of their former royal trappings.

But Irwin also visited the slums in major cities, despite his staff's suggestions that "places like this aren't for the likes of you." He did not intend to be an autocratic ruler who delivered fire and brimstone whenever the people of India sought an improvement of their conditions and better civil rights. In this, he set himself up for a high-wire balancing act that would be a challenge to maintain in any circumstances, let alone facing the unusual political movement that Gandhi was leading.

There was a rule book—a harsh one—when it came to confronting a violent uprising. But what was one to do when facing a rival who simply marched defenseless through the countryside and peacefully said, "No more"? The easy answer would have been to seize Gandhi and to have him jailed. The tax collector in whose district the march was taking place urged this very action. Irwin firmly said no. The arrest of Gandhi's lieutenant Vallabhbhai

Patel by that same official had already given the Indians another cause célèbre. Stopping the march might very well incite riots in Ahmedabad and its surrounding villages. Instead, Lord Irwin decided to maintain his chosen course of action and to not arrest Gandhi. Writing to King George V, who was the titular emperor of India, Irwin explained that there was still hope the march would be a "fiasco."

Irwin suspected that the journey to Dandi was only the first stage in Gandhi's plan, and that Gandhi's arrest would usher in the second stage: furthering popular support. The third stage would come in the shape of a mass nationwide campaign. If Irwin could preclude the second stage by holding back from arresting the movement's leader, then the whole affair might fizzle away.

Still, as viceroy, he needed to take at least some precautionary action. He sent sizable reinforcements of police, soldiers, and munitions to Gujarat and offered rewards to local Indian leaders for maintaining their positions in the face of calls by Gandhi for their resignation. Finally, he ordered his officials to send bands of workers to the seashore to begin clearing and destroying the natural deposits of salt. Such was his position that it seemed less trouble to defy nature than Mohandas Gandhi and his column of marchers.

The relentless journey continued for Gandhi and his followers. Wednesday, March 19, over a week into the march, was the hottest day yet, and the swirl of dust in the increasingly barren landscape almost overwhelmed the marchers throughout the six miles to the village of Ras. Then they forged ahead roughly the same distance to the tiny village of Kankapura beside the Mahi River.

A pair of new marchers had joined the column a few days before, bringing their number to a total of eighty-one. One was a twenty-year-old student whose younger brother was already in the ranks. He had grown up in the ashram and, on the invitation from the Mahatma, had hurried from his university to meet them on the road. "So, Shankar has risen to the occasion," Gandhi said on his arrival. "No wonder we shall win swaraj when there are earnest lads like you ready to sacrifice."

The other marcher was twenty-six-year-old Kharag Singh—a convicted murderer. Singh had stabbed to death a wealthy Calcutta merchant who had repeatedly abused a young Nepalese girl. Singh surrendered himself to the authorities and asked for the maximum sentence, but after a public outcry, he had been released. In his youth, he had stayed at the Satyagraha Ashram, and, when he heard of the march, he sent Gandhi a letter asking to be included "to make amends" for his crimes.

Uproar followed Singh's arrival. How could he be allowed to join this peace march, many asked. Gandhi wrote out his thoughts during rest periods along the road, and in an article titled "We Are All One: God Is Present in All of Us," he explained that the "sin of one is a sin of all. And hence it is not up to us to destroy the evil-doer. We should, on the contrary, suffer for him. From this thought was born the idea of satyagraha."

There was plenty of suffering to be had simply under the fierce sun that bent the air into mirages in the distance. The marchers draped cloths over their heads to ward off the heat. One wrote, "The unbearable heat of the sun, hot gusts of wind blowing over us, flies adding to the discomfort—the only relief from this unbearable situation was sleep and forgetfulness." With each step, they grew wearier. The once military-like column had devolved into straggling clumps of seven or eight individuals that stretched out a quarter mile. Some were so fatigued they had to take short rides on the oxcart. Everybody had blistered feet, many suffered episodes of fever.

The marchers found little peace and their leader even less; his time and attention were constantly in demand. Gandhi usually awakened before the 4:00 a.m. call so he could tend to his correspondence in the quiet, even though the moonlight was frequently so dim he could not read his handwriting. On the road, his pace tended to quicken if weariness, aching joints, or the press of onlookers felt like they might compel him to stop. Often it was momentum alone that carried him forward. He suffered a persistent low fever and needed oil to be rubbed on his legs each evening to keep away the cramps. But he kept going.

The Mahi River, a tidal river on the Gulf of Cambay, was over two miles wide by Kankapura. They could only cross it during the high tide, which was not until late that night. At 10:30 p.m. that moonless night, they moved down a desolate sandy valley toward the Mahi riverbank. To reach their boat, they had to trudge down the riverbank through knee-deep mud for several hundred yards before climbing aboard.

The crossing took over an hour before the shallow waters on the opposite bank stopped the boat at least a half mile from the shore. Again, they had to plod through thick sluggish ooze to reach the far bank. At one point, Gandhi became stuck and could not budge a foot. He had to be carried on the back of one of his fellow marchers. The marchers reached the riverbank at 1:00 a.m. and soon after collapsed into sleep.

Shortly after midnight, Jawaharlal Nehru arrived in Kankapura by car, planning to join the river crossing. He wanted to meet with Gandhi before the Congress committee gathered in Ahmedabad on March 21 to determine the campaign's next steps. He realized he was too late: The marchers had already left by boat. Nehru commandeered a makeshift timber raft and headed through the waters toward the opposite bank. With the tide ebbing, the raft stopped far short of the riverbank and, like the other marchers, Nehru had to trudge a fair distance through the mud to reach the shore and locate the sleeping marchers.

When Gandhi awakened at 4:00 a.m., he and Nehru walked

together to the next village stop at Kareli. They discussed progress so far. It was hard to get a sense of whether the march was gathering momentum. At each stopping place, the size of the crowds that assembled, the funds raised, and the number of resignations had roughly leveled off. In contrast, there were daily, headline-grabbing reports about the Salt March in almost every newspaper in India—and in many foreign papers as well. The viceroy had even begun to censor some of this news, starting with a ban on newsreel films about the march. However, the catalyst that would widen the scope of the campaign—the arrest of Gandhi and his fellow marchers—had, surprisingly, not yet happened. The Indian National Congress needed a backup plan if Gandhi remained free.

After their discussion, Nehru received the directions he needed from Gandhi. If Gandhi was not arrested, the nationwide satyagraha would commence as soon as the marchers reached Dandi and publicly broke the salt laws on April 6. Nehru gave a short speech of encouragement to the other marchers and then motored the two hundred miles north to Ahmedabad. There, he gathered with others in the Indian National Congress, including his father, Sarojini Naidu, and the old resistance lion, Abbas Tyabji, at a rally on the grounds of a local university. "The time for empty talk [is] past," Nehru declared. Gandhi alone could not carry the "whole burden" of the campaign. Once Dandi was reached, they needed to be ready with local leaders and volunteers throughout the country to break the salt laws and to launch "civil disobedience on a mass scale."

Not long after these plans were resolved, Nehru was back on the road. This time, his father and Naidu traveled with him, and they met up with Gandhi again in the town of Jambusar. Again they walked the dusty road together for a spell before Jawaharlal Nehru had to leave, to return to planning the nationwide campaign. It was the last time Nehru would see Gandhi during the march. For the rest of his life, he would remember the sight of the Mahatma, staff in hand, at the head of the column. "Here was the pilgrim on his quest of truth," he later wrote. "Quiet, peaceful, determined and fearless, who would continue that quest and pilgrimage, regardless of consequences."

Chapter 7

One day followed the next on the journey south to Dandi. Wake up at 4:00 a.m. Prayers at 4:20. Washing, breakfast, and packing up camp by 6:00. March a half dozen miles. Stop by 10:30 at the next village on the way. Unpack. Relax. Clean the Untouchables' quarters. Lunch. Spinning. Diary-writing. Prepare for the village meeting. Leave by 4:00 p.m. for the next leg of the march. Walk another five to six miles. Prayers, often in a field along the way. Arrival in the dark at the next village. Set up camp. Dinner. Attend visitors. Public meeting. Sleep.

Manilal was managing the burden well. "God has given him a strong physique," Gandhi wrote to his daughter-in-law, Sushila. "And he is all simplicity of heart. Nothing makes him unhappy. There is no limit to his courage. How can such a person suffer? He has been looking after me." It was the kind of praise a son craves from his father, and it was rare for Manilal to receive it.

Each new leg of their journey brought further doubt. At one village, the locals asked the marchers if they could please stop somewhere else. At another, only the sparest of crowds showed up to greet them, or later to listen to Gandhi's speech. The marchers' days were spent trudging through deep muddy gullies or facing the brutally hot sun without any recourse to shade. One in five of the marchers was now ill, whether from fever, boils, or feet so blistered they struggled to continue. Some were beginning to complain about the meager amount of food they had to eat at each stop.

On March 26, they reached Broach, a large town. Colorful khadi banners decorated the path to the local ashram, where they were able to rest. Manilal was impressed to find a crowd of twenty thousand present for Gandhi's morning address. After a series of poor receptions, this was a bright moment, made brighter by the attendance also of Sarojini Naidu and Abbas Tyabji. Gandhi delivered a well-received speech on how their movement would need more than just Hindus to succeed. "Mussulmans, Parsis, Christians, Sikhs, Jews"—all were essential. "The cruel salt tax is no respecter of persons . . . This is the fight undertaken in the name of God and for the sake of the millions of paupers of this country."

In sharp contrast to the reception in Broach, in Sajod the following day, Gandhi was pained not only by the sparse welcome but also by the absence of khadi wearers. He feared that freedom would come very slowly to India if this town was any indication.

On the way to the next town, the column of marchers disassembled into bunches stretching out over a long distance. It was true that the road was little more than a dirt rut, and that many times they had to struggle through dried-up cotton stalks and patches of cactus, but Gandhi still expected his marchers to maintain a line. He sensed that many of them were losing morale. Several moaned about the dust and heat. The day before, at Broach, two of them had slipped away to the town bazaar to have ice cream—a minor dietary offense but a sign that order was breaking down.

At the evening prayer meeting, Gandhi upbraided his marchers for their complaints and lack of discipline. He reminded them that discipline was important not only for the individual but also for the movement. Self-rule for India would not come without it. Any other path was unacceptable. The Dandi pilgrimage provided the opportunity for each marcher to exercise and embrace the power of satyagraha. A failure in self-discipline in the smallest of things—griping about the food, not spinning enough, or failing to maintain one's diary (an effort in personal examination)—was nothing less than a betrayal of their freedom movement. Having spent decades shaping this philosophy, he was now immovable from it—harsh though he could be.

There was something else gnawing at Gandhi's sense of justice. With each day of the march that passed, he grew increasingly unsettled by how much he and his fellow marchers were demanding of the villages they passed through. On March 28, they needed to cross a river, and the villagers built a small bridge with bamboo poles for them. That night, as they came into Umrachi, several local volunteers lit their path with kerosene lamps. Gandhi appreciated their willingness to help, but he knew that the oil was expensive for them. He also learned that the residents of Umrachi had trucked in supplies of milk and that they had used what meager supplies of flour they had to make bread for him and his marchers. The fact that they were imposing such a burden on this poor village upset him greatly.

There was worse to come. The following day, in the village of Ertham, Gandhi learned that his drinking cup had broken and that his assistant had requisitioned two drinking cups from the village to replace it, which was a huge imposition on their limited resources. Then he discovered that these villagers too had brought in supplies for the marchers—a haul of fresh vegetables and fruits, including mangoes, grapes, squash, and tomatoes—in spite of barely being able to put food on their own tables. That all of these gifts were for him and his marchers while the people of Ertham were destitute caused Gandhi to burn with shame.

That evening, the breaking point came. As they entered the village of Bhatgam, the marchers were met by a local youth carrying a heavy kerosene lamp with which to light the path. Prodded by his boss, a wealthy nationalist, the youth had to run to keep up with the marchers. Gandhi was appalled. At 9:30 p.m., he stood on a dais in front of a few thousand people, his marchers directly in front of him. More kerosene lamps illuminated the gathering. "Tonight," he began, "I propose to make a confession and turn the searchlight inward."

He then spoke about how he and his marchers had faltered in their discipline and how they had caused undue burden on the

villagers. "We are marching in the name of God. We profess to act on behalf of the hungry, the naked, and the unemployed." If his column of marchers were taking from the poor and requiring an "unconscionable burden," then "what right had I to write to the viceroy the letter in which I have severely criticized his salary which is more than five thousand times our average income?"

Gandhi's tone grew more strident and pained. "These lights are merely a sample of the extravagance I have in mind. My purpose is to wake you up from torpor. Let the volunteers account for every [cent] spent. I am more capable of offering satyagraha against ourselves than against the government . . . If then we do not quickly mend our ways, there is no swaraj such as you and I have put before the people." One by one the kerosene lamps around the meeting place were extinguished, casting the surroundings in darkness.

As he finished his speech, Gandhi almost broke down in tears. "From my outpouring, you may not infer that it shall weaken my resolve to carry on the struggle. It will continue no matter how my coworkers or others act. For me there is no turning back whether I am alone or joined by thousands. I would rather die a dog's death . . . than that I should return to the ashram a broken man." He apologized to the villagers for not using their charity well and told the gathering to regard him as a "wretch" and to "shun" him.

When Gandhi left the stage, Manilal was shaken—and inspired—by the words. Everyone was. If the marchers were to be worthy of swaraj for India, they would have to steel their discipline in heart, body, and soul.

The day before Gandhi's electrifying speech, Sir Frederick Sykes, governor of Bombay, took a train to New Delhi to meet with the viceroy. Now forty-three years old, Sykes had begun his career as a civilian clerk before helping to oversee a tea plantation in British Ceylon. Unhappy with this life, he had then volunteered for the British Army and had fought in the Second Boer War in South Africa (1899–1902), spending some of that time as a prisoner of war. Later, avidly interested in aeronautics, he learned to fly and was deployed in France during World War I as an officer in the Royal

Flying Corps. Sykes ascended through the ranks to become chief of staff. By the end of the war, when he turned to politics, he had earned numerous medals.

In 1928, Sykes was appointed governor of Bombay. He remained a military man at heart, with conservative views, and believed that force of arms was most often the best course of action—and the earlier the better. Of all the members of Lord Irwin's governing cabinet, Sykes faced the highest level of political unrest in his area of control, which included Gujarat, where the Salt March was taking place. As far as he was concerned, the viceroy was taking a "deplorably weak" approach to Gandhi, and Sykes suspected that Irwin did not see the value in maintaining the empire. Sykes wanted Gandhi and his marchers arrested and imprisoned for the long term, and he wanted any further rebellion squashed before it could gather steam. Otherwise, he was convinced, it would quickly grow out of control.

This Sykes made very clear to Irwin when he met with him in private at Viceroy's House on March 28. "The line of least resistance" must not be maintained, he stressed. He discounted reports from undercover police following the marchers who described how Gandhi was fatigued and "dejected on the whole with the reception he received." These reports also suggested Gandhi might be suffering from heart disease and high blood pressure, making it unlikely that he would complete the distance to Dandi. Sykes refused to depend on this outcome—nor was he convinced that the march would fizzle into nothing as the British press insisted it would. A *Daily Telegraph* editorial had described Gandhi as "engaged in a futility which grows daily more humiliating."

In Sykes's view, Gandhi was causing "great excitement" among the villagers. Each day Gandhi continued was a victory in its own right. People were sympathetic to the cause of the Salt March—and were becoming increasingly so as the "old man" battled the heat and distance for no benefit of his own. Village officials continued to resign. Volunteers were lining up to join the cause, thanks to Jawaharlal Nehru and the Indian National Congress. Sykes believed it likely that resistance to the land tax would follow, and then a nationwide civil disobedience campaign against the Raj. After all, Nehru was publicly calling for it. Sykes suspected such a campaign would turn violent, as previous nationalist movements in India had done.

Sykes also used the argument that international attention on the march was growing. Every day in the United States, newspapers were publishing articles and photographs about the events. Some observers there likened the Salt March to the American Revolution's Boston Tea Party. "Gandhi Opens Drive for India Self-Rule," declared the *New York Times* in one lead article. Sykes's conclusion was that all this uproar must come to an end.

Once again, Irwin refused to take immediate action. Worse—from Sykes's point of view—the viceroy had decided not to arrest Gandhi if he broke the salt laws. Irwin instructed Sykes that the police should arrest other Congress leaders once they violated the law—but not the Mahatma. There was a good risk he might die in prison, and they must not give him the "halo of martyrdom."

For Irwin, it was imperative to "keep the political temperature as low as possible." Like Gandhi, he understood that violence on the scale of Jallianwala Bagh or Chauri Chaura could break out otherwise. Irwin remained convinced that support for the salt campaign was limited almost exclusively to the area of the march. And, he argued, even if support widened beyond Gujarat and the military was brought to bear in the situation, British Army numbers were too limited to quell a mass uprising. In the district of Surat alone, where Gandhi was now headed, there were 5.5 million people and two British officials with a police force of 742 officers responsible for keeping law and order in the area. That was simply not enough. Finally, Irwin believed that a peaceful political agreement was still possible. To his mind, the use of military force would be an outright "admission of failure" on his part. That said, he conceded that were Gandhi to die on the march, it would provide "a very happy solution" to the whole "silly salt stunt."

Sykes left the palace without having secured a commitment from Irwin to take action. All he could do was to continue to send troops into the area, to intercept and censor letters between nationalist leaders, to protect salt-producing works, like the one at Dharasana, to destroy each new batch of salt left by the tides around Dandi, to watch, and to wait. Only if the "situation deteriorated fast," Irwin advised, should they alter course.

The day after Gandhi's "searchlight" speech, March 30, the mood in the column of marchers was much brighter. Discipline in the line was strong. The willingness to sacrifice themselves to the cause had never been higher. After a late-morning stop, the marchers continued ten miles through a scorching sun to Delad, where they erected their camp in a grove of tamarind trees. That day, the marchers spun at their charkas and taklis for a longer time than on any previous day. They also restricted their diet and did not accept food from the village market. Their new resolve was plain.

For Gandhi's speech that night, attended by close to six thousand people, only candlelight illuminated the field. The crowd's expectant silence gave Gandhi's soft words even more impact. "Although I was agitated yesterday and still am, I have not lost my peace; the fiery words of love which I had directed toward my friends were not regarded by them as such . . . Yesterday I did not find the outer and inner peace which I find in today's assembly."

The tide was turning. With each day that passed, the marchers met Gandhi's call for more discipline, and the people in each village were inspired by their presence. Granted, the district in which they were now crossing was already supportive of the nationalist movement, but the degree of enthusiasm was more than just that. Muslim communities, largely absent from the early gatherings, began to appear for his speeches. India might well get the freedom Gandhi professed they deserved, if they all rose to the call.

There was a sense now that Gandhi and his band would indeed make it to Dandi. Despite rumors to the contrary, the government was clearly not planning to arrest the movement's leader. "The tiger does not appear," Gandhi said at one stop, baiting the British to come and get him.

On April 1, ten thousand people welcomed the column of marchers as it neared the city of Surat. By evening, when Gandhi spoke by the riverbank, there were ten times that number—an undulating sea of people, all wearing khadi. Several village officials and police offered their resignations from the Raj. Donations of jewelry and money amounted to a small treasure. "There is no alternative but for us to do something about our trouble," Gandhi began, loudspeakers booming his voice across the crowd. "And hence we have thought of this salt tax. You may say it is a godsend. It is so beastly and inhuman that through salt the government taxes even little children and young girls . . . This is an inhuman law, a satanic law."

The following morning, the marchers left the city like a conquering army. Colorful banners and strings of leaves hung from balconies and across arches. Flowers were thrown at their feet. Such was the heat and press of people that it was almost difficult to breathe. It was with some relief that they returned to the countryside and to another stretch of walking. At a rest stop, Gandhi advised his marchers of what they faced in Dandi, at the end of pilgrimage. There would be little water or food. Their diet would have to be further restricted to some puffed rice and broth. "You shall get used to this for we have to lead austere lives," he said. They should also expect to face government forces who might wield water cannons or firearms. "We have prepared ourselves for death," Gandhi said. "Not one of us will retreat."

After crossing the Mindhola River via a makeshift bridge of unhitched bullock carts, the column of eighty-one headed to the village of Navsari, thirteen miles away. This was one of the longest stretches in an already long march. They arrived in town on the evening of April 3, under a sky of gold and purple, to what one observer labeled a "right royal reception." Most of those in the vast crowd that followed them in the streets wore khadi. The Indian National Congress flag flew from rooftops, and fabric bunting dangled between houses. An estimated fifty thousand people attended Gandhi's speech outside the public hall. Enthusiasm was at a "high pitch."

There to witness the reception was Jawaharlal Nehru. Any lingering fears he might have had over the success of the Salt March faded that night. As he later wrote, "Salt suddenly became a mysterious word, a word of power . . . spreading like prairie fire."

Chapter 8

It was the last day of their journey: April 5. After almost a month on the road together, Manilal and the other marchers had become a band of brothers. They had spent the previous night in Matwad, a village eight miles from Navsari. From there it was only a three-mile walk to Dandi. Manilal ate breakfast, said his prayers, and prepared to leave. He had good reason to feel proud of his effort over the long trek. While others had fallen ill or broken their discipline, he had remained steady, earning the continued praise of his father.

The marchers filed out of Matwad, followed by a crowd of well-wishers. Trees formed an archway over the road, and rhesus monkeys swung from branch to branch over their heads. After twenty minutes, they reached a marshy plain that opened out like a fan toward the coastline and the village of Dandi. As one marcher wrote, "the murmur of the sea was loud and musical and could be heard from a distance." A small bridge crossed over a trickling channel, then a much longer wooden bridge stretched over the floodplain. Each day, during high tide, the Arabian Sea spread its waters across the plain. When the waters receded, puddles of salt water were left in a myriad of dimples and depressions. The hot sun then evaporated the seawater, leaving behind a crust of salt. This was the treasure they had been sent to gather.

The government, in its efforts to destroy these salt deposits before the marchers arrived, had sent work crews to level the plain—but this was a Sisyphean task. Every time the tide went out, it left fresh scatterings of salt in the hollows. Now the marchers looked upon the salt deposits with "childish glee." With each step, their excitement grew. Any of them could easily have bent down and collected some salt in his hand. But their lawbreaking was scheduled for the following day.

Through creeks, mud, and silty earth, they marched onward. Eyewitnesses wrote almost mythic chronicles of the scene, now in the last hours of their journey, particularly of the Mahatma: "The red sun had just risen over the roof of the railway station, and his bare face and body was golden and transfigured in the light of morning. It did not seem to me he was using his staff to any purpose. He was not particularly leaning upon it. He seemed strong, lean like a lathe and fleet of foot . . . The breathless walk made you see how urgent and downright and final was his call and his message. He did not tarry for the roadside honors from devotees. He passed on after a lady had placed a kum-kum on his forehead and a man had showered rose-water."

The pace Gandhi was setting through the marshy grounds was indeed fast. He maintained something between a walk and a run, eating up the distance to Dandi in an hour. There was no time for weariness, blistered feet, or feeling faint from the sun. If Manilal had ever doubted the will of his father, he must have doubted it no longer. Only his own remained in question.

Set atop hummocks of dry ground and separated by the sea and a surrounding spread of marshland, the village of Dandi resembled an island—especially at high tide. Home to 460 people, mostly fisherfolk, it was little more than an assembly of a dozen houses and roughly a hundred makeshift shacks. A long, wide beach sloped down from the village to the metallic blue waters of the Arabian Sea, where, along the seaside, there was a handful of spacious bungalows built by the wealthy, most from Bombay, seeking respite from the city heat. The village seemed as insignificant an endpoint for their pilgrimage as the salt tax had been a rallying point for independence.

They neared Dandi at 7:30 a.m., buffeted by sea breezes. Some straggly cows meandered the sandy lanes. A score of men and a handful of boys—all wearing khadi—greeted them and accompanied them into the village, where several hundred people were waiting to celebrate their arrival. The welcoming committee sang songs and threw flower petals at their feet. Sarojini Naidu, Abbas Tyabji, and several other Congress members were there to greet them as well.

Soon after arriving, Gandhi retired to a two-story seaside bungalow owned by Nizamuddin Vasi, a wealthy Bombay merchant who had invited him to stay there. Now, at the march's end, a posse of newsmen descended. Between meditating and reading scriptures, Gandhi welcomed journalists to speak with him. From the very inception of the march, it had been essential to spread the word and to garner support beyond the narrow corridors where they were traveling.

Sitting cross-legged on a mattress, wearing only a loincloth, and often spinning cotton as he spoke, Gandhi delivered his message to Indian and foreign journalists alike. *Why choose April 6 to break the salt laws?* That was the day, eleven years before, when Gandhi launched a nationwide strike against the British Raj to protest the oppressive Rowlatt Act. "The 6th of April has been to us, since its culmination in the Jallianwalla Bagh massacre, a day for penance and purification," he told the Associated Press. *Are you expecting to be arrested?* "I know nothing for certain," Gandhi explained to the reporter from the *Daily Telegraph*. "And there are no outward signs of my impending arrest, but generally when the British authorities are most quiet is just before they mean to strike." *At what point will you stop the campaign? What if violence breaks out?* "As long as the current regime remains standing, no measure, whatever it is, will suffice to appease me," Gandhi explained to the reporter from *Le Journal*. "I will go to the end, whatever happens, without any kind of truce . . . The British do not have the courage to stop me, but they'll have to do it sooner or later. That day, I will not wish them harm. I will pray to God to change their hearts." At the end of each interview, Gandhi typically gave the visiting reporter a strand of khadi he had spun himself. Then they were ushered out to make way for the next. At one point, Gandhi scribbled a statement to an American supporter that would later become famous: "I want world sympathy in this battle of right against might."

For hours, Gandhi received a steady flow of visitors, including Tyabji and Naidu. If he was arrested, Gandhi told them, he wanted Tyabji to take leadership of the campaign. And if Tyabji was taken by the British, then Naidu would step into command. The two accepted.

Nearby, in huts beside a cluster of mangroves, the other marchers took time to relax. Many strolled along the black-sand beach or dunked themselves in the warm waters of the Arabian Sea. With every passing hour, hundreds of Indians flowed into the area, either on foot or off buses from Navsari. Their numbers quickly overwhelmed the resources of the seaside village. Over a hundred British officials were also present in Dandi, including excise inspectors and policemen. They kept a close eye on the encampment. Beyond that, it was unclear what their intentions were.

Gandhi emerged from the bungalow at 6:30 p.m. and threaded his way through the swelling crowds that had gathered to hear him speak. He stopped by an enormous banyan tree near the local primary school. The sun was setting, and the sky glowed a kaleidoscope of color. Embraced by the long, leafy arms of the tree, Gandhi began one of the most momentous speeches of his life: "When I left Sabarmati with my companions for this seaside hamlet of Dandi, I was not certain in my mind that we would be allowed to reach this place . . . That I have is in no small measure due to the power of peace and nonviolence; that power universally felt . . . Tomorrow we shall break the salt tax law. Whether the government will tolerate that is a different question."

Many in the crowd thought this would be Gandhi's last speech as a free man. This fact gave his every word more import. The sky darkened further.

"This movement," Gandhi continued, "is based on the faith that when a whole nation is roused and on the march, no leader is necessary . . . If you brothers and sisters come forward as true volunteers and commit civil disobedience of the salt law no matter what force the government threatens to use against you, and if you do whatever else you may be required to do, we shall have in us the power to attain in a single day what we hold to be our birthright." When Gandhi finished his speech, he returned to the bungalow, where he wrote letters, had his weary feet massaged with oil, and then went easily, and soundly, to sleep, as was his habit. Tomorrow would bring the next, more perilous stage of his campaign.

The next morning, April 6, as the sky lit up with the approaching dawn, Gandhi came out of the bungalow and down its front steps. Barefoot, and wearing only a wrap of khadi and a loincloth, he made his way down the beach toward the water. His band of marchers and a crowd of over four thousand people surrounded him, and beside him walked Sarojini Naidu.

Naidu cared not for the ascetism Gandhi imposed on himself and his followers. She thought it unnecessary for India to gain its freedom. But her earlier skepticism about the march and the protest against salt had long since disappeared. She could not deny the enthusiasm the action had stirred up in Gujarat and throughout India. The fact that Gandhi had tapped her to lead the movement if he, then Tyabji were arrested was an honor that moved her profoundly.

Despite the government staying its hand throughout the march, Naidu and many others feared that Gandhi's arrest was imminent. They wondered whether the 150 policemen gathered outside the bungalow would allow him to break the salt laws. Surely, they would pounce at the last minute and haul the Mahatma away before he could collect his symbolic pinch of salt?

Gandhi crossed toward the gentle surf. Nobody impeded him. Naidu and the marchers followed closely behind. Just before he reached the sea, Gandhi stopped and announced, "This religious war of civil disobedience should be started only after purifying ourselves by bathing in the salt water." He shed his khadi wrap and, wearing only his loincloth, started into the lukewarm waters of the Arabian Sea. There was a stir in the air, and the waves out in the distance were choppy. Given the low tide, it took a fair spell of walking through the shallow surf before he reached a depth that even covered his knees. A pair of satyagrahis bookended him, lest the waves topple his slight frame. Finally, Gandhi lowered himself into the sea, disappearing for a moment before rising again.

As he made his way out of the surf, the other marchers dunked themselves and then followed Gandhi back onto the black sand. With the sun beginning to creep onto the horizon, the scene of white-clad figures had a particular majesty to it. Gandhi wrapped his khadi shawl around his shoulders again and headed back in the direction of the bungalow. Always conscious of time, he wanted to break the salt laws at 6:30 a.m. sharp. Again, Naidu walked at his side. The police kept to the edges of the crowd, clearly not intending to interfere. A hundred feet from the bungalow, Gandhi stopped in a wide furrow that had been created by the tides. His marchers gathered around him. With each passing second, the sky brightened on the horizon.

Then Gandhi bent down and scooped up a handful of mud mixed with a scattering of salt. "With this salt, I am shaking the foundations of the empire," he declared.

"Hail, lawbreaker!" Naidu called out. There were shouts of "Mahatma Gandhi ki jai!" ("Victory to Mahatma Gandhi!"), and many other marchers stooped over and collected their own fistful of earth and salt.

Then, with mud clinging to his feet up to the ankles, Gandhi returned up the steps of the bungalow, a broad smile on his face. Shortly afterward, he met with the press and issued a statement: "Now that a technical or ceremonial breach of the salt law has been committed, it is now open to anyone who would take the risk of prosecution under the salt law to manufacture salt wherever he wishes and wherever it is convenient." Gandhi also gave voice to

something that was very dear to Naidu: "I am preparing a message for the women of India who, I am becoming more and more convinced, can make a larger contribution than the men toward

the attainment of independence. I feel they will be worthier interpreters of nonviolence than men, not because they are weak . . . but because they have greater courage . . . and immeasurably greater spirit of self-sacrifice."

A reporter asked Gandhi, "What do you intend doing afterward?"

"Oh," Gandhi said, "I shall continue to manufacture illicit salt."

All through the morning and afternoon, Gandhi's marchers and hundreds of volunteers, men and women alike, carried brass pots into the surf and filled them with seawater. Back at the camp, others were stoking up fires, and they boiled the seawater in pans. Deposits of salt were left behind after the water had evaporated. In the surrounding creek beds and hollows along the coast, many more scraped the earth for salt, piling it into mounds. Not once did the police intervene.

After making another speech to his followers at 4:00 p.m., Gandhi retired to the bungalow. Naidu, who went with him, wrote a letter to her daughter: "The little lawbreaker is sitting in a state of 'Maun' [silence] writing his article of triumph for *Young India* and I am stretched on a hard bench at the open window of a huge room that has six windows open to the sea breeze. As far as the eye can see there is a little army—thousands of pilgrims who have been pouring in since yesterday." In her letter, Naidu complained about the food and the sticky salt bogs into which she sank up to her ankles, but she wrote that she wished her daughter could have been with her to witness the day's incredible events. Through his simple act, Gandhi promised to ignite a firestorm that would sweep the country. As his third-in-command, Naidu must have known that one day she would have to take the lead.

Chapter 9

Jawaharlal Nehru was seven hundred miles north of Dandi, in the Punjab city of Gujranwala, when he heard that the salt laws had been broken by Gandhi, as planned. He heralded the news at a satyagraha conference: "The 6th of April is a memorable day for India. Eleven years ago, on this very day, the whole of India declared a historic hartal as a protest against the Rowlatt Act. Today, again, on the very same day, Gandhi ji and his volunteers have reached Dandi sea-coast and broken the salt laws. This day will remain a red-letter day in India."

Over the past week, as president of the Indian National Congress, Nehru had toured hundreds of miles of countryside by car, spoken at twenty-two mass meetings, and addressed over 200,000 people—rousing them to join the campaign. The fruit of his efforts, given force by Gandhi's acts in Dandi, quickly took shape. On April 7, waves of volunteers harvested salt and staged protests against the Raj. In Bombay, a rally filed through the streets, closely watched by mounted police. Nationalist songs rang out, and the satyagraha leaders were garlanded with flowers as they reached the city's shoreline. There, they collected pots of seawater and boiled them until there was salt ready to collect by the pinch. "Lusty cheers" rose from the surrounding thousands, then the salt was taken back to the Indian National Congress headquarters to be auctioned off to raise funds.

That evening, on the golden sands of Chowpatty Beach, fifty thousand people celebrated breaking the salt laws. Bombay's Congress committee leader, Kurshed Nariman, announced that the crowds would be out the next morning to produce more contraband salt. Similar scenes played out in Calcutta and New Delhi, as well as in towns, villages, and hamlets all along the vast Indian coastline. Where there was no salt to be collected, people boycotted foreign cloth and liquor shops, stopped rail traffic, openly read seditious literature in the streets, and resigned from their posts serving the British government. The sale of contraband salt was commonplace as well.

From the Satyagraha Ashram, Gandhi's secretary, Mahadev Desai, championed the campaign in Ahmedabad. Writing to Nehru, he included a few crystals of salt in the envelope that had been collected by the Mahatma at Dandi. "I am addressing meetings daily the likes of which I never addressed before in my life," Desai noted. "They are all models of orderliness and silence. Volunteers are coming in at great numbers . . . If this thing goes on, as indeed it will go on, my days too are numbered." Nehru knew to what he was referring: the likelihood of arrests.

These began in Surat, on the evening of April 6. Ramdas Gandhi, the third-born son of the Mahatma, who had been recruiting volunteers while the march proceeded to Dandi, was arrested and sentenced to six months' hard labor for possessing five pounds of illicit salt. Dozens of Congress leaders were taken the following night, including Nariman, the Congress committee leader. His sentencing, which was also swift, led to a citywide strike the following morning. Bazaars and markets closed. Schools emptied. And thousands marched in the streets, banging drums.

Most confrontations with British authorities were civil. However, in Aat, only four miles from Dandi, where the police tried to forcibly seize the salt collected by volunteers, one of the volunteers suffered a slight injury. It was provocation enough that the whole town came out—men, women, and children alike—to join in panning for salt.

Never one to miss an opportunity to teach a larger lesson, Gandhi rushed to Aat the next day and declared, "Ours is a war of love in which we have to suffer too . . . Do not let go of salt when the police tries to snatch it from your hands. So long as your wrists are intact, do not let your fists be loosened. Your fists will acquire the strength of iron if you have faith in satyagraha."

Soon after, the police raided the Indian National Congress headquarters in Bombay. They demolished the pans of evaporating salt water on the rooftop, then tried to raid the party's offices. Several women stood in their way. "You may arrest us or do whatever you like," said one. "But you shall not make us desert our post of duty."

The police overpowered the women, but not once did the resisters forget their discipline and raise a hand or their voices in violence.

Still on his travels, Jawaharlal Nehru openly tempted the British Raj to arrest him. He called on students to suspend their studies and join the campaign. On April 10, he led a group of satyagrahis in selling contraband salt in Allahabad. So enormous were the crowds that the police had no chance of reaching him. Later, he auctioned off the salt. "Let all who dare stand up against British imperialism and plunge into the fight," he told the press. "Forward, then, to the goal of freedom. India expects every Indian to do his duty." Every hour, the civil disobedience movement grew in size and scope, and the rosters of satyagraha leaders who had been imprisoned grew longer. Nehru expected that he would be next.

The first seven days of protest, action, and widespread civil disobedience against the salt laws had exceeded even Gandhi's own lofty expectations. He had kept mostly to the towns around Dandi, giving speeches, attending interviews, writing letters and articles, and brazenly and openly harvesting salt. He courted arrest constantly, yet it did not come—despite persistent rumors of his imminent imprisonment.

The Indian and world press were also keeping a close eye on the situation, and news about Gandhi's peaceful political movement was splashed across newspaper headlines from Bombay to Berlin, Paris, London, and New York. Still, it was not enough. The viceroy and the British government clearly still believed that the campaign would "slow down to die a natural death" if Gandhi remained free.

No arrest. No martyrdom. No riotous uproar. Gandhi decided that he would force their hand. "The real heat is still to come," he wrote to a Congress leader.

Apart from the lack of any widespread participation by the Muslim community, Gandhi was pleased with the level of resistance throughout the country. The mammoth numbers coming out in Bombay, Calcutta, and New Delhi to protest the salt laws were "beyond words." He also welcomed the many arrests. For every satyagrahi taken, a dozen or more came to stand in their place. Already, he had begun sending away his marchers to shepherd efforts across the country. Manilal was the first to go, leaving for Surat to take the place of his arrested brother, Ramdas.

Gandhi believed that women joining in large numbers could turn the tide, and by encouraging them to join the cause, he ushered in the first truly universal mass movement in India. On Sunday, April 13, at 3:30 p.m., he joined five hundred women on the beach in Dandi for a special conference. Many had walked the twelve miles from Navsari to hear what he had to say. There, under a blazing sun, he delivered a speech inviting them to join the struggle. The speech drew from an essay he had written shortly before the gathering: "If by strength is meant moral power, then woman is immeasurably man's superior. Has she not greater intuition, is she not more self-sacrificing, has she not greater powers of endurance, has she not greater courage . . . If nonviolence is the law of our being, the future is with women."

Gandhi urged the female volunteers—and their sisters across

India—to step forward and focus their attention on shutting down two key industries: liquor and British cloth. If they succeeded in picketing and bankrupting these businesses, it would hurt the Raj's income almost fifteen times as much as the rebellion against the salt tax. In this fight by the "women's army," Gandhi said, "we shall have become purer and added to our strength, and then it will not take long for us to secure swaraj." One conference attendee asked what they should do if attacked. Gandhi answered simply that they must "court suffering."

The next day, April 14, brought great news: Jawaharlal Nehru had finally been arrested—at a railway junction outside Allabahad. After a hasty trial, he was sentenced to six months in prison. Leaving the courtroom, Nehru shouted, "Keep smiling, fight on, and see it through." Gandhi telegrammed congratulations to Nehru's father, Motilal. "Have just heard Jawaharlal arrested. I greet you and Saruprani as happy parents. Jawaharlal has earned the crown of thorns."

The reaction to the imprisonment of the Congress's president was immediate and immense in scale. If the youth of India needed another reason to join the ranks, they had it now. In a letter published in the nationalist press, Gandhi appealed to them directly. "It was impossible for the government to ignore the young president and an ideal patriot . . . This arrest should cost the government its existence. Will the youth of the country realize this hope and now leave their schools and colleges and work for independence?"

In Bombay, twenty thousand people clad in khadi proceeded to the Esplanade Maidan, a triangular park in the heart of the city. Sarojini Naidu spoke to the gathered masses from a platform. Her prominent presence was yet another sign of the rising role of women in the independence movement. Naidu told the crowd how on a recent trip to America she had described Jawaharlal as "the symbol of young India." His arrest, she said, should be an "occasion of joy for the nation . . . Today, all creeds and castes were forgotten, and there was only one word on the lips and in the hearts of all, and that was freedom of the mother country."

Amid this developing crisis, Lord Irwin was on a ten-day official tour of what the *Times of India* called the "wild and woolly" northwest frontier between India and Afghanistan. No viceroy before him had visited many of these areas, and the terrain was so unnavigable that he traveled mostly by airplane. On April 15, he landed in the Valley of Swat, a jaw-dropping setting beside a towering range of snowcapped mountains called the Hindu Kush. One of the early centers of Buddhism, it was an area of sweeping alpine meadows and untamed forests—a welcome break from the stifling heat of New Delhi. There Irwin met with an assembly of local tribesmen in their leader's tent and presented that leader with a knighthood of the British Empire. Such were the duties of the viceroy.

But try as he might, even in such a remote location, Irwin could not escape the spiraling disorder taking place across the country. While in Swat, he received a sobering letter from Bombay governor Sykes, who continued to press him to take a firmer hand with the resistance movement: "There is no doubt that Gandhi has a great emotional hold as evidenced by the numerical support of his demonstrations and the popular enthusiasm, largely among the younger generation, and, increasingly, among women and girls, which has been more than expected." Sykes also noted that "Gandhi has scored a certain degree of success in attaining his objective to reach the masses [and] that the law can be defied if sufficient concerted action is brought."

The British government in India was disturbed by the reaction to Nehru's arrest. Across the country, in cities big and small, shops, bazaars, and market exchanges closed their doors. Those that did not were picketed by volunteers, especially tobacco and liquor stores. Children stayed home from school. Buses and trains remained in their central stations and depots. Street marches, many made up

solely of women and students, blocked traffic. Bonfires of foreign cloth sent plumes of smoke into the air. And everywhere that it was possible to get away with it, satyagrahis manufactured and sold contraband salt.

In several cities, the police tried to break up these assemblies. When the people refused to disperse, police rushed them, wielding long batons called lathis, causing numerous casualties. In a Calcutta suburb, two trams were trying to leave their depot when a mob blocked their way. The crowd urged the drivers to abandon their jobs, and when they refused, violence broke out. Stones were thrown at the tram windows, and the lines were blocked with dustbins. Elsewhere in the city, rioters poured gasoline onto other trams in one of the main thoroughfares and set them ablaze. When the fire brigade tried to reach the scene, they were met by a mob. Police and army troops were called into the area. Force met force, and numerous people were sent to the hospital. While Calcutta saw the worst of the rioting, there were sporadic outbursts elsewhere, including in Karachi.

Lord Irwin had always feared that violence would spring from any resistance campaign, no matter how peaceful Gandhi intended his rebellion against the salt laws to be. He wrote to his father, explaining what he considered the heart of his problem: "I am anxious to avoid arresting Gandhi if I can do so without letting a 'Gandhi Legend' establish itself that we are afraid to lay hands on him." What he had hoped was that his orders to arrest everyone *except* Gandhi would isolate the leader and quell his movement's impact. The British prime minister and his government supported this view.

According to the propaganda of Irwin's home country's press, he was right to chart this course. "The policy of the government has upset Gandhi's calculations," declared the *Daily Telegraph*. As a British correspondent wrote from India, all the fuss about Gandhi and salt was much ado about nothing. "It'd be possible for a traveler to journey from Ballard Pier [in Bombay] across to Calcutta or up to Delhi without realizing that anything was wrong."

Willful denial might have been playing out in loyalist papers, but the international press refused to overlook the significance of events. Cairo's *Fatah* newspaper wrote, "One single man sets the example to all the countries of the East which is held totally suppressed . . . Gandhi is the standard of heroism in national leadership." France's *Le Journal* dubbed his course of action "the Campaign of the Hindu Messiah." The American press was no less subtle. *Time* magazine labeled Gandhi a "saint" and "statesman" who utilized "Christian acts as a weapon against men with Christian beliefs."

The Reverend John Haynes Holmes, one of the founders of the National Association for the Advancement of Colored People (NAACP) and the American Civil Liberties Union (ACLU), a man whose sympathy Gandhi had openly courted, proclaimed in a sermon, "This immortal Indian, as mighty in spirit as he is feeble in body, is not only incomparably the greatest man in the world today, but one of the ten or a dozen greatest men who have ever lived."

So not only was Irwin losing control of India, he was losing control of global opinion about the British Empire as well. Two days after the first riots took place, in Calcutta and Karachi, Irwin arrived in the summertime headquarters of the British Raj, at Simla, in the foothills of the Himalayan mountains. That same day, Gandhi gave an interview to the *Free Press of India* agency about the riots. Any hope the viceroy might have harbored that the recent violence would convince Gandhi to call an end to the campaign was quickly dashed. Even though the rioting "harms the struggle," Gandhi said, "the struggle has to go on unchecked. If nonviolence has to fight people's violence in addition to that of government, it must still perform its arduous task at any cost. I see no escape from it."

Reports streamed into the Viceregal Lodge in Simla that the unrest was deepening by the day. More marches. More defying the salt laws. More resignations. More women and students joining the campaign. More picketing of liquor and British clothing stores. More arrests and assaults by the police. More riots. More violence. In Bengal, on April 18, a group of sixty revolutionaries disguised as soldiers raided the police armory in the port town of Chittagong. Several British troops were killed. Later, the group cut telegraph wires into the city and derailed a train in the countryside. Gandhi spoke of his abhorrence of these acts but said that, in his consideration, they were perpetrated by a "small body of men who do not believe in nonviolence." He made very clear that there would be "no suspension of the fight."

Shortly afterward, in Peshawar, a march turned unruly, and Indian Army troops opened fire on the crowd, killing over thirty people. In response, the mob attacked several armored police cars, setting them on fire with gasoline and burning their trapped occupants alive. Irwin ordered in reinforcements only to later learn from confidential reports that the Indian infantry troops refused to go to the area and shoot "unarmed brethren." This was mutiny, a very grave sign for the viceroy.

Although most of the movement remained nonviolent, the incidents in Chittagong and Peshawar were a step too far. Irwin instituted martial law in the former and called up loyal forces to crush the rebellion in the latter. As for Gandhi, Irwin was slowly coming around to the fact that he must be arrested. Governor Sykes insisted on this course of action, cabling late in April that "Gandhi's exemption from arrest is having an important effect in strengthening the civil disobedience movement. His arrest would tend to check it by removing the brain which guides it." This advice came on the heels of a letter sent from Sir Malcolm Hailey, governor of the United Provinces and one of Irwin's self-declared "wise men" of Indian affairs. Although Hailey had previously advised caution in arresting Gandhi, he now recommended that "they had already waited too long and should act speedily now."

Even so, Irwin remained reluctant to imprison a man who most Indians believed was more saint than politician. If the uprising after Jawaharlal Nehru's arrest was any indication, the public outcry after the Mahatma was arrested would be massive indeed.

Irwin also regretted that events had arrived at this state of affairs. Writing C. F. Andrews, a former Anglican priest and British supporter of Gandhi, Irwin noted his frustration with Gandhi at having not seriously pursued negotiations before the march: "I cannot bring myself to understand how he has been right to throw away what seemed a golden opportunity for men of goodwill to work together."

Then Gandhi staged a provocation that removed any last doubt from Irwin that he must take action against him.

Chapter 10

On April 26, Gandhi traveled by motorcar through the Gujarati countryside, passing through several villages on his way to the city of Bulsar. Along the route, people lined the streets, cheering him as he passed. When he arrived at his destination, where he was due to give a speech, the townspeople welcomed him with bags of contraband salt and garlands of khadi.

In his speech, Gandhi railed against the Raj, as he had in many speeches before. He also celebrated the string of arrests, praised the number of women joining the movement, and promised that greater sacrifices would have to be made for swaraj to be won. Gandhi knew the outbreaks of mob violence in Calcutta and Karachi—as well as the organized attacks against the British in Chittagong—were putting the movement in jeopardy. As he had explained in his weekly column in *Young India*, "Pledged as we are to strict nonviolence and truth, any manifestation of force or fraud or violence on our part means a victory for the devil in us."

Unlike in the past, Gandhi had no intention of calling an end to their efforts in the wake of this violence. There were two chief reasons why he was willing to continue. First, the majority of the movement remained peaceful; second, his volunteers proved willing to face not only arrest but also cavalry charges, lathis, bayonets, and even bullets to realize their independence—a fact that Gandhi believed "opened an entirely new and a proud page in our history." Even so, he had been mulling over how to raise the stakes in the fight against the viceroy and the British Raj. He told an ashramite in a letter, "I am conceiving the last move that must compel decisive action. But it is all in God's hands."

After speaking in Bulsar, Gandhi traveled on to Chharwada, where he ended his day. He had chosen the hamlet because it lay only a mile from Dharasana, a major producer of salt. There, spread out over a vast, treeless, three-mile-square plain surrounded by an iron-wire fence, were the Dharasana Salt Works. To manufacture salt, workers channeled seawater into large rectangular depressions in the ground and then let the sun evaporate it into a brine as the sand and clay settled out. This brine then flowed into a series of evaporation pools until the workers had separated out the salt—mostly sodium chloride (common table salt). They then raked the salt into baskets that they carried to the massive cones of sparkling white salt, big enough for two people to stand atop. These cones dotted the plain, evidence of the enormous quantities of salt being manufactured by the state-controlled works.

From the platform where he stood to speak to the gathered crowd of Chharwada villagers, Gandhi could see the haystack-size mounds of salt in the distance. Now it was time to reveal his plan:

You may call me a salt thief, but only when we take possession of the salt beds of Dharasana. What is there in picking a seer or two of salt from here and there? Even the government must be wondering what a childish game we are playing. If you mean to play the real game, come out and loot the salt beds of Dharasana . . . From that one day we will proceed to serious business.

Gandhi then looked to the crowd. There were only three hundred people in attendance in the small village, but he invited them all, "brothers and sisters" alike, to join him in the raid.

If these government men seize our finger, we will offer the wrist, and if they seize the wrist, we will offer the shoulder; and if they seize the shoulder, we will offer our very neck . . . Do not think it will be two or three years before the raid takes place.

THE SALT MARCH

An old man like me, past sixty years of age and nearing death, cannot speak in terms of years. I can speak only in terms of a few months, and, if you give me your cooperation, a few days.

Gandhi may have been addressing only the small number of Chharwada villagers, but he was directly challenging the British Raj more strongly than ever.

A thousand miles away from Chhadwara—a journey that would take almost two days by train—was Simla, the summer headquarters of the viceroy and his administration. Set in tiers on the steep, pine-forested hills in front of the Himalayas, Simla seemed a different world altogether from the arid Gujarati coastline. At seven thousand feet above sea level, a cool mist hung in the air. Birds twittered in the tulip trees, and butterflies flitted about the rainbows of bougainvillea that spilled over the many terraced walls. All in all, the city had the feel of a splendid mountain resort town.

In the "English Quarter," there was a bustling grand avenue called the Mall, the cream-colored steeple of Christ Church, the Gaiety Theatre playing the latest import from London, and a shopping district of British-branded businesses: Piccadilly House, Oxford Stationery, Thomas Cook, and Lloyds Bank. Villas and charming cottages abounded, most with well-tended gardens of roses, acacia trees, and rhododendrons. In the streets and parks, nannies tended their young British charges, couples strolled with tennis rackets under their arms, horseback riders wearing stylish jackets clip-clopped down the cobblestones, and well-suited clerks and uniformed military attachés moved about with purpose.

Farther down the hillside was the Lower Bazaar. Packed with

stalls selling everything from glassware to fried food to sweets, the warren of twisting, narrow streets often reeked of sewage runoff from above. In this busy quarter lived the laborers, rickshaw drivers, maids, cooks, and washerwomen—and there was scarcely a European to be seen. One Western journalist described the scene with barely veiled racist overtones, typical of the times: "The crowds flow in and out . . . with an amazing and frightening variety of types, costumes, voices, and gestures. There are stocky Mongols with bony faces; tall patriarchs with noble features; thickly bearded officials draped in togas pulled back over their shoulders; fine aesthetes with narrow waists, tight in silk tunics; beggars with heavy leather satchels; and the arrogant wealthy with turbans of all shades and shapes, embroidered caps, and red fez."

On the afternoon of April 27, 1930, a stream of khadi-clad satyagrahis came parading through the bazaar. They were following a rickshaw carrying Vithalbhai Patel to the train station. An elderly statesman, Patel had resigned his position as head of India's Central Legislative Assembly two days before. The white-bearded former Congress leader, whose views had moderated with age—unlike those of his brother Vallabhbhai Patel (arrested before the Salt March began)—now declared: "My country has embarked on a life-and-death struggle for its freedom. The civil disobedience movement organized by the Congress under the leadership of Gandhi, the greatest man of modern times, is in full swing. Hundreds of the most prominent of my compatriots are already determined to sacrifice their lives if necessary . . . My place should therefore be with [them], shoulder to shoulder, and not in the chair of the President of the Legislative Assembly."

Meanwhile, Lord Irwin met with his senior aides in the imposing graystone Viceregal Lodge, perched high on a promontory over Simla and guarded by a unit of Gurkha, some of the most fearsome soldiers in the British Indian Army. Everything in his study, from his ornately carved wooden desk to the paneled Burmese teak walls, spoke to the great wealth his countrymen had amassed from Britain's rule over India.

Dispatches from throughout the country poured into Irwin's office: The numbers of Indian women joining the movement continued to rise. Gujarat was all but lawless. Peshawar remained in a mutinous state, even after Irwin had dispatched troops. More and more moderates were siding with the "swirling mob." The Muslim community might follow. And now Gandhi was giving a string of bombastic speeches about "a raid" at Dharasana and how it was "better to die than remain slaves."

Many in Irwin's government feared that if he did not do something fast, India's place in the British Empire, and the magnificent wealth it contributed to its coffers, would be in dangerous jeopardy. Already that morning, he had rebuked Vithalbhai Patel in an open letter, saying that he could "only hope that you and those with whom you are once again to be openly associated may come to realize how grave a wrong you do to India by rejecting the way of peace."

More severely, Irwin reinstated the Indian Press Act of 1910, a censorship law first established to prevent the "dissemination of sedition and incitements to violence." In his announcement, he stated that the civil disobedience movement was "rapidly developing, as all reasonable men foresaw, into violent resistance to constituted authority." Therefore, the problem must be addressed for what it was: "a dangerous emergency." To this end, members of the British Parliament in London were already calling for harsher, more repressive measures. Their argument focused on how even Gandhi was referring to his campaign in terms of "raids" and "battles" and "soldiers" and "war." If war it was, these politicians argued, then the British Empire knew how to respond. The *Daily Express* agreed: "The day that a policy of repression is decided on will mark the end of the crisis . . . The rebellion would be crushed." A French reporter interviewed a British official in Simla, who threatened, "We Englishmen take a very long time to get angry, but once we are angry, we become pigs."

Irwin hesitated to give in to these passions. His job was to broker a peace and to restore law and order so that India could get back to business. However, it was clear that the time to arrest Gandhi had come at last. It might spark more unrest, but at least Gandhi's army of volunteers would be without a leader. Further, the Indian public would see that nobody in the Raj was above arrest and that the British—and he, the viceroy, their representative—were the ones in power.

On April 29, Irwin instructed Frederick Sykes, the governor of Bombay, to issue the arrest warrant under an old ordinance that gave the government the right to imprison indefinitely, without trial, any individual considered a threat to public order. The law had gone unused for almost three decades (when it was invoked to arrest a murderer). Preparations needed to be made for the arrest and the specific timing orchestrated to lessen any uproar, but it was decided. Gandhi must go.

On May 4, in Surat, Gandhi gave another provocative speech, saying, "This is my last throw, and I am out to lose my all for the liberation of India." That evening, he returned to Karadi, the village where he had established his headquarters. It was only a few miles from Dandi, and almost as remote and small, but it had better access to roads. Sitting in his reed hut, located beside a mango tree, Gandhi drafted a new letter to the viceroy. As in the letter he had written before launching the Salt March, he again delivered an ultimatum.

"Dear Friend," he began. "God willing, it is my intention . . . to set out for Dharasana and reach there with my companions and demand possession of the Salt Works." Gandhi proposed three ways in which this raid could be avoided: (1) remove the salt tax; (2) arrest him and his party; or (3) sheer brutal force. If force was to be the answer, he warned, "According to the science of satyagraha, the greater the repression and lawlessness on the part of authority, the greater should be the suffering courted by the victims. Success is the certain result of suffering of the extremest character, voluntarily undergone."

It was after midnight when Gandhi at last lay down on his cot and closed his eyes. Two satyagrahis were sleeping on the ground beside him. A short distance away, dozens of followers, several of whom had made the march from the Satyagraha Ashram to Dandi with Gandhi, slept out under the stars. It was a humid night, and even though clouds illuminated by the moon drifted overhead, there was very little stir in the air.

At 12:45 a.m., there was a bustle of movement in the encampment. Feet stomping. The clinking of metal. Hushed whispers. Sentries around the perimeter had been told to bang pans if they perceived any threat, but no warning signal came. Before anyone was aware of their presence, two British officers had led a platoon of thirty Indian policemen to Gandhi's hut. Having surveilled the Karadi camp over the previous days, they knew exactly where to go, and they formed a cordon around the hut. The officers were armed with pistols, the policemen with rifles. They had come expecting trouble.

Inside the hut, a pair of flashlights shone onto Gandhi's prone figure. He stirred and rolled over, still unaware of the threat. Finally, one of the officers barked, "Please wake up!" Gandhi awakened with a start. He propped himself up on his elbows and stared at the officers. "Have you come to arrest me?" he asked.

"Yes," said H. V. Braham, district magistrate of Surat. "Your name is Mohandas Karamchand Gandhi?"

Gandhi swung his legs off the cot. "Do you mind waiting until I brush my teeth and wash my face?"

Surat's police superintendent, G. S. Wilson, checked his watch and reluctantly agreed. As Gandhi readied himself, a warning bell finally rang through the camp, and Gandhi's followers approached the police cordon. Several tried to reach their leader, but the police held them back.

Ever the lawyer, Gandhi took a break from brushing his teeth to ask why he was being arrested. "Is it Section 124-A of the Indian Penal Code?" He was disappointed to learn that he was not being arrested for sedition, like so many freedom fighters before him. Instead, he was being taken under a written order from Frederick Sykes, Governor of Bombay. Braham read from it. "Whereas the Governor-in-Council views with alarm the activities of Mohandas Karamachand Gandhi, he directs that said individual should be placed under restraint under Regulation XXV of 1827, and suffer imprisonment during the pleasure of the government: and that he be immediately removed to the Yerwada Central Jail."

"Thank you," Gandhi said. Having heard the detail of the order, he understood that he would not have the opportunity of a trial. He instructed his eight-year-old grandson, Kanti, to prepare his bedding so he could bring it with him to jail. Then he told one satyagrahi to take charge of his papers and another to retrieve for him a pair of hand spindles so he could spin yarn in prison.

Braham and Wilson were both impatient to leave and urged Gandhi to hurry up. Rather than indulge them, Gandhi asked his fellow Salt Marcher Narayan Khare to lead the camp in a Hindu hymn. Plucking an ektara, Khare sang, "Oh Rama! Lord of the Dynasty of Raghus! Thou, an ideal king, an ideal husband of the ideal wife Sita, Thou are verily the Redeemer of the fallen and the sinful!" While Gandhi and the others joined in the chant, the two British officials anxiously checked their timepieces yet again and urged, "Please hurry up!"

"Have you any message for Kasturba?" someone asked as others bent down to touch the Mahatma's feet in a show of respect. Gandhi's wife was away, leading the picketing of liquor shops in another town. She would not be surprised to learn of his arrest, which she had been expecting for almost two months now. "No, I have no message for her," he said nonchalantly. "Tell her she is a brave girl."

He was then taken out of the camp by Braham and Wilson. A police constable carried the two satchels and a bundle of clothes that Gandhi was bringing with him. He walked steadily and happily away. At last the British Raj had followed through on the arrest he had long been courting.

The two officials kept a close eye on their watches as they reached the line of police trucks. There was a schedule to keep. It was 1:10 a.m., and the Frontier Mail train traveling between Ahmedabad and Bombay would be waiting for them at a level crossing outside Karadi. As soon as they boarded the red-and-yellow train, the brakes released and it steamed off into the night. Five and a half hours later, it rounded a bend and came to a screeching halt at a rail crossing outside the town of Borivili, thirteen miles from Bombay. Dawn was just beginning to break, and the smoke from the train's engines billowed into the lightening sky.

Gandhi's arresting officers wanted to avoid potential crowds that might be waiting at a suburban station. What was more, all telegraph and telephone lines had been blocked, to prevent news of the arrest from spreading. Nevertheless, two intrepid journalists, Negley Farson from the *Chicago Daily News* and one from the *Daily Telegraph*, had been tipped off about the relay point and were waiting beside the railcar when the carriage door opened. An attendant set a stool down on the ground, and a moment later, Gandhi appeared in the open doorway of the train. He stepped onto the stool, then onto the railside, looking altogether full of cheer. He was greeted by Inspector Cordon, the deputy superintendent of police of Poona, where the jail Gandhi was being brought to was located.

The train's other passengers gazed out their windows, wondering why they were being delayed at this wayside location. To their amazement, they saw Mahatma Gandhi under police guard.

"Any word, Mr. Gandhi?" the *Daily Telegraph* reporter asked.

"Shall I say them now—or shall I wait?"

"You'd better say them now . . . In a few minutes you'll be on the way to prison."

"Tell the people of England and America," Gandhi said, "to realize what is being done on this morning. Is this liberty?"

Gandhi was then escorted to a large yellow Studebaker. Its windows were veiled with cloth to keep away prying eyes and its engine was already running to make for a swift departure. Gandhi climbed into the back seat, sandwiched between Inspector Cordon and another policeman. Moments later, the car eased away into the

dark, followed shortly after by the jarring screech of the train as it continued on to Bombay.

At 10:45 a.m., the Studebaker arrived at Yerwada Central Jail outside Poona, a hundred miles southeast of Bombay. Gandhi thanked Cordon for his gentlemanly treatment, then entered through the tall gates of the high-security prison.

Chapter 11

The following day, May 5, in response to Gandhi's arrest, Sarojini Naidu led a march that snaked for two miles behind her through Bombay. It started at Congress House, the headquarters of the Indian Congress Party, and made its way toward the Esplanade Maidan. As news of Gandhi's imprisonment spread, people poured into the streets to join them, causing traffic jams. Most shops, markets, and schools remained closed. Posters across the city called for a general strike, and workers at the textile mills and railways downed tools and came out in overwhelming numbers.

The procession was a vast sea of white khadi. Although Naidu's feet hurt, and although she was tired after days of campaigning, she refused to take a car to the Maidan. When she arrived at the park, over 100,000 more people met her. She marveled at the outpouring of support for whom she called "The Little State Prisoner." Stepping up on the platform, she knew well the movement needed to raise the stakes and to build pressure on the Raj. Yet she was fearful that events might spiral into violence without the Mahatma's leadership to temper people's anger. All the way to the Maidan she had heard shouts of "Down with the red monkeys!"—a slur against the British.

Naidu began her speech in English. She wanted the American journalists in the audience to know what her people felt. "We are the custodians of Gandhi's unfinished dreams," she began, explaining that they were gathered to congratulate him on his arrest. "Stone walls do not a prison make. We have the history of our prisons bound up with the history of our civilization . . . So what did it matter if this fragile little man was put behind the prison bars? The prison was merely the accidental shell of that great and glorious spirit. The Gandhi who will survive through the generations to come was the Gandhi who had given the lesson, simple and supreme, which paraphrased in the Bible was 'Love thy neighbor as thyself' . . . Let us carry on his message of love and nonviolence by splendid discipline, action and unity."

Across India, similar demonstrations took place. In the holy city of Benares, while mourning families and Hindu priests carried on the age-old ritual of burning the bodies of the dead to release their souls to heaven, a troop of white-clad satyagrahis descended the wide sandstone staircase to the banks of the Ganges, shouting, "Mahatma Gandhi ki jai! Long live Gandhi. He is arrested. Gandhi is arrested." Quickly, a strike paralyzed the city.

Similarly, in Calcutta, Delhi, Jalalpur, Navsari, Ahmedabad, Simla, and Solapur, huge crowds took over the streets. Negley Farson, the *Chicago Daily News* reporter who had witnessed Gandhi's transfer to prison, reported on one such parade:

> *For over an hour, I watched the great mass of Hindus, spattered with Muslims, walk past me. Flags fluttering, nondescript bands playing; banners of swaraj. A great snake of white speckled with sections wearing red turbans; the orange-colored saris of women picketers; carts with placards pulled by hump-backed idol-eye sacred cows. The Hindu cries were like the sound of heavy surf. Gandhijiki Jai, Gandhijiki Jai!; and then in a sinister rhythm, "Boycott, boycott!"*

After the Bombay rally, Naidu traveled to Allahabad to meet with other Congress leaders and decide on next steps. She was kept closely informed on the state of the demonstrations and the continuing strike. Some had indeed turned violent, and—depending on which newspaper was read, or report heard—it was caused either by mobs attacking the police or by the police attacking peaceful protesters. Arrests spiked, and shots were fired in Calcutta and several smaller cities to disperse the crowds. Dozens were killed in Peshawar, where troops backed by tanks and machine guns took back the streets.

The next major step in the campaign for freedom was not Naidu's to make. It was Abbas Tyabji who was charged to lead the Dharasana Salt Works raid. Gandhi's arrest had made Tyabji the leader of the movement, with Naidu now second-in-command. Seventy-six years of age, and instantly recognizable for his shock of white hair and heavy beard, Tyabji was known as the "Grand Old Man of Gujarat." On the night of May 11, he was in Karadi, all set to leave the next morning for a three-day trek toward the saltworks, twenty-six miles away.

Sixty volunteers, including several of the original Salt Marchers, were going with him. There was excitement and possibility in the air. Everyone expected that this escalated operation against the Raj was bound to meet stiff—and likely violent—resistance. There were local reports that six trucks of armed policemen had traveled from Surat to Dharasana to await them. But they also knew that the harsher the crackdown from the Raj, the more followers would join the fight for India's freedom and the greater the sympathy that would be won.

That evening, Surat's deputy superintendent of police, Mr. Kothawala, came to meet with Tyabji. Kothawala carried with him a written warning of the "serious nature and consequences of the course on which he proposed to embark." The government, the notice advised, was "resolved to stop the commission of the said offense by all the necessary means." Tyabji made it clear that his "highest duty" was to lead the raid. He explained that nothing would alter him from the course he was set upon. Kothawala, whose own grandfather was friends with Tyabji, asked respectfully, "Why should you put yourself to this hardship at this time of your life?"

"You youngsters think that you have the sole monopoly of all big undertakings." Tyabji smiled at the deputy superintendent. "I am eagerly waiting to see when you yourself will come forward to take your place at my side."

At 4:00 a.m. the following morning, Tyabji awakened to the prayer bells and went to join the other marchers. "In thy name, O God, we launch forth today. Give us strength to go on, to endure all sufferings with a smiling countenance and a heart singing."

Two hours later, the band of sixty gathered in a column. Kasturba Gandhi was there to smear a saffron tilak on Tyabji's forehead, much as she had done on her husband's brow before he left Satyagraha Ashram two months before. "May God give you strength to fight the government," she told him.

With Tyabji in the lead, the satyagrahis advanced through a field, singing hymns. Some had begged Tyabji to make the journey by car, but he made it clear that he would be marching. Following behind were over two thousand supporters from the surrounding villages. A few hundred yards from the camp, they reached the road heading south toward Dharasana. There they were stopped by the district magistrate, Mr. Braham. He was accompanied by several hundred policemen, all carrying rifles and lathis. Immediately, they surrounded the column of marchers. Braham announced that they were an "unlawful assembly" and commanded them to turn back. Tyabji shook his head. No. The magistrate turned to the volunteers, asking them to withdraw. "No, no," called back the satyagrahis.

"I shall then have to arrest you," the magistrate said.

Tyabji gestured toward the policemen and their weapons. "Do it by any means. You can use them too if you like."

"No, we have no such intention," the magistrate said.

Tyabji and his volunteers were escorted onto buses that were already waiting on the roadside. All the while, the local villagers who were with them cheered loudly. As the buses pulled away, Tyabji shouted to those on the roadside, "Carry on the struggle! Carry on the struggle!"

Now it was Naidu's turn to spearhead the movement. There would be no long march to Dharasana. The government had proved how easily it could stop them at a distance. Instead, she directed her volunteers to travel directly to the saltworks from where they would launch their raid.

Behind the old stone walls of Yerwada Central Jail, Gandhi occupied a two-room cell with a covered terrace and a small yard. He had been provided with a bed and a mosquito curtain, a table and chairs, two bookshelves, and his own toilet. There was even electricity. Compared to his previous stays in prison, in both South Africa and India, it was comfortable living.

He kept to a rigid schedule—much like his routine at the ashram. Early to rise, he brushed his teeth and washed himself. He prayed twice a day, for an hour each time. He took two naps: one at 8:00 a.m., the other at noon. He walked the yard for an hour, then read for two. He spent three hours preparing and eating his meals, which typically consisted of milk curds, tomatoes, boiled cabbage, and pumpkin. He added a bit of salt for good measure. He spent five hours a day spinning. At night, he slept out under the open sky.

In his thoughts—and in his correspondence—Gandhi didn't focus on the resistance movement. He could do nothing for it from his cell and so left it outside the prison walls. This sense of anasakti (nonattachment) was something he had learned long ago from the Bhagavad Gita. He dedicated himself now to his "jail life": improving his spinning, memorizing scripture passages, and writing encouraging messages to his followers.

On the same day police troops arrested Abbas Tyabji and his companions, Lord Irwin made an unexpected public statement from the Viceregal Lodge in Simla, in which he announced his intention to move forward with the Round Table Conference in London that would discuss the Indian governmental reforms that Gandhi had "spurned." He set the date for October 20.

Irwin blamed the recent "mob violence" and "armed murderous raids" squarely on the shoulders of Gandhi's civil disobedience movement and said that government forces had, "with regret, but inevitably," needed to take action to face "this growing menace to the well-being and security of the Indian public." He added, "I recognize that at the present time there is a widespread desire throughout India to see real political advance, and I have learned to love India too well to relax my efforts to assist [her in this effort]."

But, he argued, Gandhi and his followers were "postponing the very things which they profess to desire for India" by their repeated lawbreaking. This must stop. The Raj would not bend.

Since Gandhi's imprisonment, Irwin was growing in confidence that he had charted the right course through the crisis. Not everything had gone perfectly, he knew. Yes, there was good reason to argue that he should have moved on Gandhi earlier. Yes, there had been waves of unrest—violent and nonviolent—across India that were disrupting normal life. Yes, the breaking of salt laws, picketing, and boycotts continued. Yes, there was some increase in international sympathy for the Indian leader. *Time* magazine praised the Mahatma for his "dignity and composure" during the raid on his Karadi camp. A hundred American clergymen cabled the British government to "seek a friendly settlement" with Gandhi. French and German newspapers praised his methods. From Panama to Sumatra to Nairobi, Indian communities called general strikes of their own in support of their people back home.

But Irwin's view of the situation in mid-May 1930 was that the independence campaign hardly threatened the British hold on India. Even though there had been an increase in the number of demonstrations since Gandhi's arrest, they were not much worse than had been experienced after Irwin imprisoned Nehru. The numerous arrests, the new ordinance against unlawful assemblies, the strict censorship of newspapers, martial law, the banning of Congress activities, and the increased presence of armed troops everywhere—all were working in his favor. With every passing day, the crowds in the streets of Bombay and Calcutta grew smaller. The cities of Peshawar and Sholapur were now under control as well, though it had required considerable force to quiet the insurgents who tried to seize power there. Back in London, Irwin's government looked on his actions favorably, pronouncing their "faith" in his leadership and their confidence that "generally the situation is well under control despite riots in various places."

As for the proposed march on Dharasana, Irwin had swiftly stopped Tyabji in his tracks and had sent battalions of troops to the saltworks in case others tried to approach it. It was one thing to march across the countryside and pick up clumps of salt-laced mud along the coastline. It was another thing altogether to raid a government-owned enterprise. Irwin believed if he neglected to stop such a move, the British Raj might as well abdicate their rule. To force, therefore, Irwin intended to respond with force.

With the Round Table Conference, Irwin hoped to sap the remaining strength from the movement Gandhi had first started with his march to Dandi. This two-pronged approach of offering peace but promising force if it was not accepted, he believed, would return calm to India—much as it had done in past uprisings against the Raj.

Manilal Gandhi was in the city of Navsari, in Gujarat, when his father was arrested. At a public meeting, under the drift of black smoke from a burning pile of British-made clothes, he called for those listening to "keep their heads cool" and to keep their anger at the government from spilling over into violence. Only by keeping to the "Mahatma's program" would they achieve their freedom, he said, swearing that his father would prefer to die in jail than come out to a "slave India."

Manilal still believed in the power of the salt campaign to deliver independence for India. His faith in his father had only deepened on their march to Dandi. Now that he and Tyabji were in jail, Manilal decided to leave for Dharasana himself. Sarojini Naidu would be spearheading the raid, but she would need volunteers on the ground who were deeply rooted in satyagraha. He was determined to be one of them.

Since April 6, and the first breaking of the salt laws, Manilal had largely been acting on the sidelines. His father sent him to replace his brother Ramdas, who had been arrested in Surat. Manilal had floundered in his efforts to manage the breaching of the salt laws there. His group of volunteers were undisciplined; they constantly failed their spinning quotas and they violated the strict diet of the satyagrahi. Gandhi had publicly reproved him and even sent another leader to take command. The act would have stung any son, but Manilal was used to such harshness from his father and wanted only, more than ever, to prove himself worthy of the cause.

Early on May 14, Manilal took a short train ride from Navsari to Dungri and then walked the couple miles to Untadi. He was accompanied by 150 volunteers, whom he had assembled throughout the Surat district. The village of Untadi was little more than a scattering of houses and a public meeting hall, but it had the advantage of being only a half-hour walk from the gates of the Dharasana Salt Works. On the approach to the government-run site was a customs house. A sign—in English and Gujarati—posted on its wall warned that Dharasana was off-limits to any public access and that trespassers would face the full force of the law.

The full force of the law was exactly what Manilal and his fellow raiders hoped they would face.

Manilal was eager to start that very day, but he tempered his impatience and instead helped set up the camp for the swelling numbers of volunteers who were converging on the village. It was blisteringly hot, with little shade other than a cluster of mango trees. This was where they pitched their tents. Naidu was expected to arrive early the next day. Then they would begin the advance, never to retreat.

Chapter 12

On her journey from Bombay to Dharasana by train, Sarojini Naidu wrote a letter to her daughter, Padmaja. "What will happen at Dharasana I do not know, but I feel greatly honored that the Little Man entrusted his special work to me . . . In case I am arrested, don't worry . . . I am sure to have a good time. Papi will fret about it so cheer him up. Goodbye my precious one."

Naidu's fellow Congress members in Allahabad had tried to convince her that leading the raid was unnecessary. She had a heart ailment, they argued. Her skills were useful elsewhere. She responded crisply, "The time has come when women can no longer seek immunity behind the shelter of their sex but must share equally with their men comrades all the perils and sacrifices of the struggle for the liberation of the country."

She arrived in Dungri station at 4:15 a.m., where she was met by a motorcar and brought to the Untadi camp. Kasturba Gandhi was the first to welcome her. "Naiduben, you're leaving us," she said gently, knowing that Naidu's arrest was imminent.

"I hope so," Naidu answered.

After prayers, she delivered instructions to the assembly of two hundred satyagrahis. They should make sure they drank a lot of water, had a simple breakfast of puffed rice and chickpeas, and prepared themselves mentally for what was ahead. She then met with Manilal and several other camp leaders to discuss strategy.

After a brief rest, she gathered again with the volunteers at 6:30 a.m. The sun had passed the horizon, and the naked blue sky promised a cauldron of a day. Most of the volunteers had cropped their hair because of the heat and a lack of washing facilities in the camp. Many carried wire cutters to get through the fences surrounding the saltworks.

Naidu addressed the fifty volunteers who would be accompanying her on the first raid. "You are carrying on the struggle started by Gandhiji," she said, her voice ringing clear. She reminded them of the attacks by the government in Peshawar and Bombay. "It rests with you to stick to the struggle in the spirit of nonviolence. Follow me in a dignified manner, be nonviolent in thought and action, and win victory in this spiritual battle." With that, she led the khadi-clad column of volunteers out of the camp.

Manilal Gandhi stayed behind. He was next in line to command when Naidu was arrested—as they all expected would happen.

The satyagrahis made their way along a rutted dirt path toward the main road almost a mile away. Government notices, strung to trees and posted on shack walls, warned of arrest for anyone carrying a weapon (even if it was a mere stick) or for assemblies of more than four people. Before the raid even began, they were in violation of the law.

At 7:00 a.m., they reached the customs house located on the road to the saltworks. A half dozen policemen stood in their path, and there were no officers present. One policeman told Naidu to wait until his superiors came. She complied for a couple of minutes but then said they would not stay there indefinitely. Moments later, she stepped around the policeman, who did not move to stop her. Straight ahead were the Dharasana Salt Works. The column had moved only a short distance when a car pulled up ahead of them and two officials—District Magistrate Braham and Police Superintendent Robinson—stepped out. Truckloads of police also converged on the scene.

Braham and Robinson approached Naidu. She stopped. Quickly, a contingent of sixty policemen assembled around the satyagrahis in a cordon three-deep. They were armed with rifles, and each carried a lathi. Nearby, reporters from several newspapers witnessed the unfolding scene. Braham advised Naidu that the only way forward was through violence. "We will stay here until Doomsday," Naidu said. "We do not intend to break the cordon by physical force." Robinson promised her that his troops would stand there as long as she, adding slyly, "We will offer satyagraha ourselves as long as you stay."

"All right," Naidu said. The stalemate began. Gradually, a crowd from the surrounding villages circled around them. The sun rose, and the air shimmered with heat. After ten minutes, a volunteer brought Naidu a chair and an umbrella from a nearby house. Her legs already felt swollen, and she gladly took the seat. Her satyagrahis remained standing, as did the British officials and their troops. After an hour, volunteers from the Untadi camp tried to bring in water. Braham refused the delivery through his cordon. The temperature was increasing with every passing minute, and there was no shade under which to escape the glowing orb in the sky. Naidu told her satyagrahis to at least sit on the road. They did, followed by the authorities, who all sat down.

More hours passed. Naidu spent most of them sitting in her chair, spinning cotton and writing letters. The first she wrote to her daughter, describing the "amusing" scene she had found herself in. Later, when local village women attempted to bring the satyagrahis water, Braham turned them back as well. Neither was any food allowed through. By afternoon, the scorching heat had become almost unbearable. Although they were near the seashore, there was no breeze. Braham and Robinson retreated inside the customs house, and Naidu and her column of would-be raiders remained under the sun. If they wanted water or food, Braham told them, they would have to step outside the cordon, but they would not be allowed back inside, nor would they be allowed to advance to Dharasana. So they all stayed out on the open road.

More and more people joined the crowds assembled to watch the standoff. They demanded to know why the police would not allow even water for Naidu and her volunteers. A policeman answered,

"These people have today come to take salt. Tomorrow they would dare plunder the treasury. Can we allow them to do that?" Some local women tried to break through the cordon with pitchers of water. The police maintained their lines, pushing them back. One of the villagers simply offered the water to the police. "You must be feeling thirsty. You too are our brothers."

Neither Naidu nor the British officials gave in. The sun set, and still they remained. Eventually, Naidu joined the other volunteers sitting on the ground and led them in evening prayers. Afterward, they sang together, their voices from their parched throats sounding tinny. Finally, at 1:00 a.m., Braham allowed food and water to be delivered to the civil resisters.

"What do you think of the food?" a volunteer asked Naidu.

"Did you expect that a lady who stays in the Taj Mahal Hotel would stay in such a place as this?" she replied.

"This is a better place," the volunteer responded. Naidu smiled in agreement.

Braham sent in a mat for Naidu to sleep on. The others lay down on the road. The night was long—and mostly sleepless. At sunrise, Naidu again led prayers for her volunteers. More songs rang out. The police maintained their cordon. The villagers who had kept vigil, squatting on the roadside, rose as well. One called out, "Oh, God is great, Naiduben must win." Volunteers from the Untadi camp arrived with bread, milk, and tea. They were allowed through the police line.

Soon after, Manilal Gandhi approached Dharasana with three

groups of fifty satyagrahis. "Follow truth, and God will bless you with victory," he called out. When the police blocked the would-be raiders, they hurried off down another path toward the saltworks. Battalions of armed troops dogged their every step, eventually halting their advance and corralling them together under careful watch. Now there were two hundred volunteers sitting on the roadside. "You won't beat us by hide and seek," a British officer told Manilal.

At 9:45 a.m., almost twenty-seven hours into the deadlock on the road, District Magistrate Braham threaded through the police cordon to speak with Naidu. It looked as though this was going to be another shadeless inferno of a day. "Don't you think, madam, you'd be more comfortable elsewhere?" he asked.

"Of course! I mean to stay here as long as I'm not arrested, or as long as I don't faint."

With that, Braham ordered her arrest. When she stood up, Naidu wobbled and almost fell back down. She was exhausted and dehydrated, and her swollen legs were numb. Once she regained her steadiness, the police led her away to a car and back to the Untadi camp. Her satyagrahis were rounded up, put onto the backs of trucks, and hauled away from the Dharasana Salt Works as well. All, including Naidu, were released from custody that same day.

The twenty-seven-hour stalemate made national and international news. Each side claimed victory. Each side derided the other. The British claimed that the would-be raiders had shown how easily they could be stopped. Those in the independence movement

declared that the authorities had cruelly kept the world-famous Nightingale of India on the roadside under the withering Gujarati heat, without food or water, yet they were too fearful to put her in prison.

This was only the first thrust at Dharasana. Other raids were also taking place across India. At the Wadala Salt Works outside Bombay, American journalist Webb Miller watched from a rocky hillside as clusters of young men in white khadi made haphazard forays toward the piles of salt. Time and again, they sprinted across muddy ditches, hurled themselves over rocks, and grabbed fistfuls of contraband salt before the police descended on them and beat them away with their lathis.

The police would seize one group of men and push and shove them toward waiting police vans only to have another raiding party strike at a different place. A British officer oversaw the defense operation, barking orders while swinging his own stave. The helplessness of the sweat-soaked British to stop the relentless raids contrasted starkly with the bright-eyed youths—some as young as thirteen—who looked like they had conquered the world whenever they collected so much as a pinch of salt. It made for an almost comical spectacle.

But these were not the revolutionary scenes Miller had traveled halfway around the world to cover. What was more, he was only one of several foreign correspondents at the Wadala Salt Works, and he was looking for an exclusive. Miller's job was to break news stories that would awe and move his readers—and maybe even make them stop and think for a moment before turning to the next article, the next page.

In early May, the telephone in Miller's London flat had rung—an urgent message from the United Press office in New York: "Go to India by first available airplane . . . cover Gandhi." The next morning, Miller was on an Imperial Airways flight to Karachi. In the short time between the phone call and takeoff, he had obtained the stack of visas he would need, along with a battery of shots for everything from cholera and plague to typhoid and smallpox. Over the next seven days, he stopped in a dozen cities and flew over fifteen countries, across deserts and seas and mountains. Finally, he reached India, exhausted and ill. While recovering from the arduous journey, Miller learned that Gandhi had been arrested and was in a prison at Yerwada Central Jail. Miller was forbidden to visit the inmate.

At thirty-nine years of age and an experienced foreign correspondent, Webb Miller's face had the tired, weathered look of a man who was rarely surprised. His brief was to report on this new method of nonviolent struggle pioneered by Mohandas Gandhi, and Gandhi was missing from the field. Miller knew he needed to find the right story to tell—and the scenes at the Wadala Salt Works were not quite that story.

After the stalemate on the road, Sarojini Naidu organized more raiding parties to breach the barriers around the Dharasana Salt

Works. The British had dug a long trench just ahead of a ten-foot-tall barbed-wire fence that surrounded the salt pans and had filled it with water. British Indian Army soldiers were posted behind the fence, all along its perimeter, and rifle brigades stood inside the stockade. On surveilling the area, Naidu half-jokingly remarked to a police officer, "You are now imprisoned behind your own bars."

Manilal Gandhi led a number of advances on the saltworks, changing tactics each time. He usually brought with him between eighty and one hundred volunteers. They would leave camp in the early morning, carrying little more than their knapsacks and water jugs. At first, they attempted direct charges down the main road, only to be repelled by the police, who arrested many of them. Their next tactic was to split off into smaller groups and march along twisting dirt paths toward remote sections of the saltworks. Occasionally, they could get a few volunteers across the ditches and through the fence with wire cutters before the police swarmed. Other times, the volunteers squatted in wait until police reinforcements dwindled in the 116-degree heat. Then they all rushed the defenses at once. They managed a few more breaches, but after a few minutes the police always pushed them back. Some attempts were made to pull down the fences with ropes. These were thwarted as well.

After three days of these raids, Manilal believed they needed a wholesale change in strategy. They needed to go bigger. Much bigger. Many of the volunteers had been arrested and were now in jail, where they immediately went on hunger strikes. The several hundred volunteers left at their Untadi camp were losing morale, and there was a risk that they might leave. If they did go, Manilal would not blame them. They were accomplishing little more than giving the British and their forces practice at repelling them.

On the evening of May 19, activist Pyarelal Nayyar approached Manilal. Nayyar had been part of the independence movement for a decade. The two had been close during the Dandi Salt March, and they had grown even closer at Dharasana. "I wish to talk to you about something," he said.

"So do I," Manilal replied.

"You see how things are taking shape. I do not like the look of them."

"I knew you were going to talk about this. Nor do I."

"Well, then?" Nayyar asked.

"We must step it up and intensify it," Manilal said, feeling excitement well up inside him. "There should be a mass raid with a minimum of two thousand volunteers to force the authorities either to imprison us all or to open up fire on us—not to play cat and mouse."

"I like it."

"And if the big guns do not listen to us?" Manilal asked, thinking of Naidu.

"In that event, let us tell them that we shall go away either to Sholapur where martial law is in force or join action somewhere else after our heart."

Manilal agreed.

"A compact, then?"

"Yes."

The two strode back to the camp and met with the other satyagrahi leaders. Naidu agreed to the escalation. Word must be spread to Bombay and elsewhere. They needed recruits—and quickly. Soon they would make their greatest push.

Chapter 13

While volunteers rushed toward the Untadi camp, Mohandas Gandhi was passing the day in Yerwada Central Jail in his usual fashion. He kept to his jail routine: praying, reading, spinning, walking the yard, and sending letters. He was rereading a biography of the Buddha, and, as he wrote to his nephew, he was "enjoying" his time in jail. From the newspapers that the prison commandant allowed, Gandhi was aware of the developing situation at the saltworks, including rumors of a major raid.

On the afternoon of May 20, British reporter George Slocombe of the *Daily Herald* visited Gandhi for his first interview since his arrest. When asked if he had "calculated all the perils" in his campaign, Gandhi said, "I have taken what has been called a mad risk. But it is a justifiable risk. No great end has been achieved without incurring danger." Of when he would negotiate with the viceroy, Gandhi replied bluntly, "Until we get satisfaction, we shall fight on until the end, and give our lives if need be in the cause of Indian freedom." If Slocombe was looking for a message from Gandhi that Naidu and others at Dharasana should back down, he did not get it.

That evening, Webb Miller was in Bombay when he received a tip that "the biggest demonstration yet" would be launched at Dharasana, early on May 21. He telegraphed Naidu, informing her that he planned on coming and asking if she could help arrange transportation at Dungri, the nearest train station to Dharasana. He never received a reply and suspected that British censors had intercepted his message. Unfazed, he boarded a northbound night train, bringing his own provisions for the journey: a half dozen sandwiches and some bottles of water.

After spending sleepless hours in a passenger compartment, being jostled around in his seat, Miller saw that the train had pulled up in the small town of Bulsar. It was 4:00 a.m. This was as close as he could get to Dharasana, the conductor told him. The authorities had instructed the train officials to skip Dungri, which was ten miles away. Miller found himself alone on the platform in the dark. He went to find the stationmaster. There was only a single motorcar in the town, the stationmaster informed him, and even if he could hire it, they would have to cross through a river whose waters were impassably high. There was no bridge.

Miller had almost given up hope when a freight train came into Bulsar. The stationmaster advised him that it would stop at Dungri. Miller hopped into the caboose with the crew, communicating with hand gestures and sharing his cigarettes. He arrived at his destination only to discover that the Untadi camp was still six miles away. He would have to walk. As the sun broke the horizon, he was still hurrying across the countryside, unsure whether he would arrive at Dharasana in time.

Even after sunrise, the moon lingered in the sky, as Sarojini Naidu stood before a throng of 1,570 satyagrahis. Volunteers had come from far and wide, answering the call for the raid on Dharasana. All of them were wearing khadi. Naidu herself was wearing a khadi robe and sandals. "India's prestige is in your hands," she began. "You must not use any violence under any circumstances. You will be beaten, but you must not resist. You must not even raise a hand to ward off blows."

The ranks of satyagrahi jostled and whispered excitedly—and nervously—to one another. This was it. The fight to the finish. They thought themselves ready—as ready as anybody could ever be to march defenseless against armed soldiers and police. "Although Gandhi's body is in prison," Naidu cried out, "his soul goes with you!" With that, the volunteers raised their voices and chanted together, "Gandhiji ki jai!"

The throng assembled into columns, the leaders of each one standing in front. They included Manilal Gandhi, ready to spearhead the raid. Abdul Kadir Bawazeer, Manilal's comrade since their days in South Africa, came forward to say a prayer. Better known as Imam Saheb, he had joined Gandhi's Phoenix Settlement outside Durban in South Africa, and he had participated in his campaigns ever since. With tears choking his voice, he called out,

"Oh God, we are all weaklings. Do not put us to hard test. We have plunged in this war in thy name. Thou art our last resort, whether thou destroyest us or savest us. Let our faith in thee be constant."

When he finished speaking, the columns moved out of the camp and down the road. Imam Saheb led the first group of five hundred volunteers. Manilal followed with the next five hundred. If he felt fear, he did not show it. This was his moment to prove himself the satyagraha warrior that his father had always wanted his son to be. He would not back down, nor would he retreat. Only wounded or unconscious would he leave the field.

Once all the columns had left the camp, they splintered off in different directions toward Dharasana. The plan was that they would advance on the salt depot from various points around its perimeter, splitting the British defenses. Some volunteers carried ropes to pull down fence posts. Others brought wire cutters. A couple dozen had stitched red crosses on the khadi draped across their chests and carried blankets that would serve as stretchers for the inevitable casualties.

They advanced the half mile in silence. Then, as they neared Dharasana, each column broke out in a droning chant in Hindustani: "Inquilab Zindabad." ("Long live the Revolution"). A hundred yards back from the ten-foot-tall, barbed-wire fences surrounding the saltworks, silence fell, and the columns halted. The piles of salt glimmered in the rising sun. The ditches in front of the stockade brimmed with a fresh supply of water. Between the trenches and the fences stood the police—local men wearing brown shorts and turbans. Each held a five-foot-long lathi in his hand. Inside the depot, there were twenty-five Indian Army soldiers with rifles. They had formed on a slightly raised knoll to provide a good line of fire on the approaching masses.

Around the works, a half dozen British Army officers oversaw the defenses, ready to give orders to repel the invaders. Already the demonstrators were in violation of the district magistrate's order that forbade any assembly of more than four people. For this alone, the British could legally move against them, arresting everybody with whatever force they deemed necessary.

Naidu arrived at the rear of the columns, one hundred yards back from the front. Webb Miller stood nearby. After marching through cactus hedges, fields of millet, and expanses of barren earth thick with dust, he had finally arrived at the camp, soaked in sweat but in time to hear Naidu's exhortation to the volunteers. He was the sole American journalist present—and the only one free to report on the situation on the ground without the interference of the Raj's censors. A crowd of roughly five hundred locals was also on hand to witness what was about to happen.

Finally, Imam Saheb made a move and directed his column toward the stockade. A British Army officer demanded they stop. They did not. Saheb and those around him waded through the waist-deep ditches and scrambled out on the other side. Mud coated their legs, and their clothes were soaked. Again came the order to halt, followed by another insisting that they disperse under the law prohibiting assemblies. Again, they ignored the commands. They continued forward, faces set.

The police tightened their grips on their lathis, the steel tips on the ends of the poles glinting in the early morning sunlight.

Several volunteers tried to lasso the stockade posts and pull them down. Yet again the police ordered them to leave. They refused—and kept going. Miller described the events in a dispatch that was published in over 1,350 newspapers across the United States and many more across the globe. His words became not only the first draft of history, but they helped change the course of that history by awakening the world to the plight of the Indian people.

"Suddenly, at a word of command," Miller wrote, "scores of native police rushed upon the advancing marchers and rained blows on their heads with their steel-shod lathis." He continued: "Not one of the marchers even raised an arm to fend off the blows. They went down like ten pins."

The dull sound of lathis striking skulls was sickening. The surrounding crowd of villagers winced at the sight of the savagery, the breath stolen from their chests. The satyagrahis understood they would be pummeled as they advanced, yet onward they came, row after row, toward the stockade. They did not cry out as the ranks of police closed on them, lathis swinging.

"Those struck down fell sprawling," Webb reported, "unconscious or writhing in pain with fractured skulls or broken shoulders. In two or three minutes the ground was quilted with bodies. Great patches of blood widened on their white clothes. The survivors without breaking ranks silently and doggedly marched on until struck down."

After a quarter of an hour, every last one of the satyagrahis in the first column had been knocked to the ground. A British officer had arrested Imam Saheb. Stretcher-bearers were trudging through the ditches to retrieve their wounded comrades. Many were dazed, some unconscious, others unable to walk and howling in pain. The casualties were too numerous for the Red Cross volunteers to handle, and it was impossible to drag the injured on their blankets

back across the water-filled ditches. Instead, they lifted the wounded onto their backs and carried them through the moat to the other side. There, the few doctors they had on hand tended to the injuries. A makeshift field hospital was assembled in a nearby thatched hut, and local villagers pitched in their assistance, their eyes welling with tears at the split skulls and savage wounds that had been inflicted on the volunteers.

Then it was Manilal's turn to lead his column into the fray. Before they crossed the ditches, he urged the volunteers to stay calm, to remain peaceful. He knew they would be clubbed down, savagely beaten, maybe even killed, but go they must. They moved forward slowly. No hesitation. No faltering. They went down into the ditch. Forced their bodies through the mud and the water. Reached the other side. Clambered out. Trudged forward. Toward the line of police that was waiting for them, lathis already cocked. "Beat them, beat them!" a police officer shouted in English, then in Hindi.

Miller chronicled what came next: "The volunteers marched steadily with heads up, without the encouragement of music or cheering or any possibility that they might escape serious injury or death. The police rushed out and methodically and mechanically beat down the second column. There was no fight, no struggle; the marchers simply walked forward until struck down. There were no outcries, only groans after they fell . . . At times the spectacle of unresisting men being methodically bashed into a bloody pulp sickened me so much that I had to turn away."

In his position at the front of the column, Manilal Gandhi was struck several times. In the head. Across the back. On the shoulders and stomach. His legs crumpled underneath him, and he fell. Then he got up again, dizzy and confused. One of the policemen grabbed him and said that he was under arrest. Manilal did not resist, but still he received several more blows to the back. The policeman hauled him away from the line and shoved him into the stockade. He had not wavered. He had shown himself a true satyagrahi, and through the crushing pain in his body and the throbbing in his head, he felt a satisfying pride that kept him on his feet.

The merciless attacks against the satyagrahis incensed the large crowd of locals who had gathered. They looked ready for a mass attack of their own. One volunteer ran toward where the British Army riflemen were assembled, baring his chest and screaming, "Shoot me, shoot me! Kill me—it's for my country." He was quickly arrested.

Naidu hurried back and forth, urging the villagers to remain calm while also encouraging the raiders to continue. Her spirited command succeeded in both aims. When another group of volunteers fell, a bloom of blood flowing down the face of its leader, she decided to change tactics and gave the order to her captains. In a coordinated action, bands of twenty-five volunteers headed across the ditches at multiple points around the salt depot and then sat down before the fence surrounding the saltworks.

"Led by a Parsi sergeant of police named Antia, a hulking, ugly looking fellow, detachments of police approached one seated group and called upon them to disperse under the non-assemblage ordinance," Miller reported.

> *The Gandhi followers ignored them and refused even to glance up at the lathis brandished threateningly above their heads. Upon a word from Antia the beating recommenced boldly, without anger. Bodies toppled over in threes and fours, bleeding from great gashes on their scalps. Group after group walked forward, sat down, and submitted to being beaten into insensibility without raising an arm to fend off the blows.*
>
> *Finally the police became enraged by the non-resistance, sharing, I suppose, the helpless rage I had already felt at the demonstrators for not fighting back. They commenced savagely kicking the seated men in the abdomen and testicles. The injured men writhed and squealed in agony, which seemed to inflame the fury of the police, and the crowds almost broke away from their leaders. The police then began dragging the sitting men by the arms or feet, sometimes for a hundred yards, and throwing them into ditches. One was dragged to the ditch where I stood; the splash of his body doused me with muddy water. Another policeman dragged a Gandhi man to the ditch, threw him in, then belabored him over the head with his lathi. Hour after hour stretcher-bearers carried back a stream of inert, bleeding bodies.*

Only a few satyagrahis escaped the beatings. The police began to force the remaining raiders away. One reluctant group was driven back by a policeman on horseback. Naidu tried to rally one last drive at the salt depot, calling the remaining volunteers onward, when a British Army officer approached and took her arm. "Sarojini Naidu," he said. "You are under arrest." Naidu shrugged off his hand. "I'll come, but don't touch me." As the officer led her away, her fellow satyagrahis and the villagers cheered. Imprisonment was always seen as a form of victory.

"By eleven, the heat reached 116 in the shade and activities of the Gandhi volunteers subsided," Miller continued in his account. "I went back to the temporary hospital to examine the wounded. They lay in rows on the bare ground in the shade of an open, palm-thatched shed . . . many still insensible with fractured skulls, others writhing in agony from kicks in the testicles and stomach. The Gandhi men had been able to gather only a few native doctors, who were doing the best they could with the inadequate facilities. Scores of the injured had received no treatment for hours, and two had died."

Vithalbhai Patel, the recently resigned president of the Legislative Assembly, arrived on the scene. Dressed in khadi, his thick white hair and beard encircling his face like a lion's mane, he sat cross-legged on the ground under the shade of a mango tree, surrounded by dozens of wounded volunteers—many wrapped in bandages. Now that Naidu and the other captains of the raid had all been arrested, leadership fell to him. "All hope of reconciling India with the British Empire is lost forever," Patel said. "I can understand any government's taking people into custody and punishing them for breaches of the law, but I cannot understand how any government that calls itself civilized could deal as savagely and brutally with nonviolent, unresisting men as the British have this morning."

Chapter 14

Almost a thousand miles away, at Simla, Lord Irwin had received a smattering of telegrams about the incident at Dharasana. One from the Bombay government read, "Police forced to repulse with lathis inflicting many casualties to volunteers." Another from British Army officers involved in the defense of the saltworks tried to cast blame on the opposing side. "Nonviolence was not so complete." They explained how a volunteer with a knife had to be disarmed by his own comrades. A policeman was "lassoed" by raiders and narrowly escaped harm. "One police officer received blow on the knee and two other contusions," the report continued. "On the whole, however, damage is small. Several volunteers received lacerations in their attempts to pull down barbed wire."

At such a remove, depending on biased accounts from his own officials, Irwin failed to understand the horrific levels of violence unleashed by the Raj on peaceful resisters at Dharasana (or their repercussions). Attempting to control the narrative of events, he sent a note to King George V. "Your Majesty can hardly fail to have read with amusement the accounts of the several battles for the salt depot." Irwin called many of the purported injuries little more than a sham—and how the raiders sought "an honorable contusion or bruise." He admitted that "as Your Majesty will appreciate, the whole business was propaganda and, as such, served its purpose admirably well."

On May 22, Irwin issued a communiqué to the press that chronicled a "mass attack" by 2,600 volunteers, who came armed with ropes and wire cutters. The limited government forces repelled the coordinated assault, the statement read, and the police exercised great restraint. "Not a single round was fired, and the only weapons used to repulse the attacks were lathis." Only three or four of the raiders were injured seriously, Irwin claimed. In conclusion, he noted, "It is obvious that the raid was skillfully stage managed with a view to secure the maximum advertisement and publicity, the motto of the organizers clearly being to the effect that unseen heroism has no press value."

British censors tried to prevent any detailed chronicles of the Dharasana raid from hitting the newspapers. They largely succeeded in India and in Britain, but they could not stop Webb Miller, the only Western reporter at the scene, from filing his report. Not that they didn't try. Once back in Bombay, Miller gave a two-thousand-word dispatch to his hotel telegraph office to send to the United Press in London. But instead of relaying the report, the telegraph staff delivered the report straight to the Bombay government headquarters, who shelved it, neglecting to inform Miller. A Gandhi sympathizer at the hotel tipped Miller off. Soon after, Miller stormed into the government headquarters and demanded that his story be delivered. One official passed him off to the next until he finally was given a hearing with the secretary of ecclesiastical affairs, of all people.

Miller threatened to fly to Persia and get his dispatch sent from there if need be. One way or the other, he insisted, his report would be published. And if the British government persisted in trying to censor him or any other journalist, he said, nobody in the world would believe a word coming from the viceroy, and maybe not even the British prime minister. His hand forced, the censor in Bombay relented and transmitted the dispatch.

Miller's report made headlines in newspapers across the United States—and beyond. Undeterred by the bad publicity, Irwin believed he could still crush the civil disobedience campaign and bring the Indian people back in line. At Dharasana and across India, his forces continued arresting civil resisters and repulsing their raids, often violently. Irwin would have preferred to negotiate a peaceful end to Gandhi's salt campaign, but he assumed he had no other choice than to restore law and order first.

After Miller's report, many Western journalists hurried to India to record the unrest and violence in vivid detail. Rabindranath Tagore, the Nobel Prize–winning Indian composer and writer, published a statement in the Western press on the effect of these horrific attacks: "Those who live in England, far away from the East, have now got to realize that Europe has completely lost her former moral prestige in Asia. She is no longer regarded as the champion throughout the world of fair dealing and the exponent of high principle, but as the upholder of Western race supremacy and the exploiter of those outside her own borders."

The afternoon after the march on Dharasana, the British converged on the Untadi camp with fifty policemen and over a hundred Indian Army troops. They declared the camp inhabitants were unlawfully assembled and gave them fifteen minutes to disperse. Several hundred did leave, but an equal number gathered together and sat down to pray. Moments later, the soldiers attacked with their lathis. Even after receiving a rain of blows, the volunteers stayed where they were. The government forces then dragged them out of the camp. Many were thrown into thorny hedges. One was struck numerous times in the head, then kicked viciously in the abdomen. He died later in the hospital. Eventually, the troops succeeded in clearing the camp.

The consequence was that more and more volunteers arrived at Untadi in retaliation. Over the next two weeks, they made several attempts to raid the salt depot. Government forces repelled them savagely. Horse-mounted soldiers were brought in to charge at the lines of volunteers. Afterward, the wounded volunteers gave statements to the press and Indian Congress representatives, detailing the atrocities they had endured.

"My one hand and one leg are dislocated as a result of lathi blows."

"A horse-hoof injured my private part . . . and I was rendered senseless."

"I was taken out and was heavily kicked twice, was given blows on the head."

"I was then dragged again till I lost consciousness."

"The policemen threw me flat into deep water and dunked me [under] about twenty-five times. Water entered in my stomach . . . I was nearly suffocated. They brought a handful of salt and thrust it forcibly in my mouth."

Finally, on June 6, the volunteers vacated the area. They had achieved their purpose, and the number of civil disobedience campaigns across the country had mushroomed. In Gujarat, resignations of Indians from the civil service hit such levels that the British could no longer control the area. In Bombay, a mile-long procession of demonstrators wound through the streets—a common sight, except this time, the marchers were Muslim. Long absent from the salt campaign in any great number, many in that community were now allying themselves with it. In almost every province, picketing of British stores became rampant, as did strikes and demonstrations that snarled traffic. Peasants refused to pay land taxes and rent. Boycotts of British goods expanded. National flags and portraits of Gandhi became ubiquitous. Thousands marched on Yerwada Central Jail, but British forces stopped them a mile away, then beat them with lathis as they sat on the road.

Huge numbers of women continued to join and participate in the movement. They were arrested in such numbers that the jail register simply noted their names as "Miss Satyagrahi." By the early summer, close to 100,000 civil resisters crowded the jails, prompting a British newspaper to publish a cartoon of the people of India crammed inside a prison. It was an illustration that mirrored a remark Gandhi had once made about how the British Raj had turned his whole country into a jail by its oppressive rule.

Something had to give.

"Mass action, even if it is intended by its promoters to be non-violent, is nothing but the application of force under another form," Lord Irwin declared at a meeting of the Legislative Assembly and Council of State in New Delhi on July 9. "And, when it has as its avowed object the making of government impossible, a government is bound either to resist or abdicate." Despite this sentiment, Irwin believed that he now had to find some way to negotiate a settlement with Gandhi and the Indian National Congress, which by that point he had all but outlawed.

The long-awaited report by Sir John Simon on potential constitutional reform finally came out in June, but it only muddied the waters further. Produced by a commission that lacked any Indian delegates, its two hefty volumes refused even the suggestion of future independence. Its proposals would have merely continued the "divide and rule" strategy that the British had followed since the East India Company first arrived on Indian shores three hundred years before.

The ingenious strategy that Gandhi had implemented with the salt campaign left Irwin in a terrible bind. If the British Raj had simply been presented with an armed rebellion, he could have crushed it with all the power of the British military. But this nonviolent movement was altogether a different animal. When Irwin stayed his hand against the resisters, he was accused of weakness by his own Conservative Party in Britain. When he acted aggressively, progressives in his country accused him of being a tyrant—as did many now in the United States.

With Gandhi's popularity and the impact of his movement gaining strength every day, Irwin decided to mediate a solution. Shortly after his joint session speech, he sent two Indian politicians—Tej Bahadur Sapru and Mukund Ramrao Jayakar, moderates both—to open talks with Gandhi and the Indian National Congress with the aim of stopping the resistance campaign. Irwin even allowed Gandhi to gather with other imprisoned leaders, including Jawaharlal Nehru and his father, Motilal, Abbas Tyabji, and Sarojini Naidu.

Sapru and Jayakar left straightaway for Yerwada Central Jail to begin negotiations. Over the next three weeks, the two moderates parlayed back and forth between the viceroy and the champions of Indian independence. Gandhi insisted that he could only accept a constitutional scheme that included the end to the salt tax, freedom for all political prisoners, and, most important, India's right to secede. Lord Irwin could only offer the promise of releasing Gandhi to attend the Round Table Conference in England, where they could discuss such goals.

On August 21, Lord Irwin received a letter from Gandhi and

the other Congress leaders. It was entitled "Time Not Ripe." They expressed a desire for a "peaceful settlement" as the joint statement opened, yet, they said, "We have come to the conclusion that the time is not yet ripe for securing a settlement honorable for our country. Marvelous as has been the mass awakening during the past five months . . . we feel that the sufferings have been neither sustained enough nor large enough for the immediate attainment of the end." Neither Gandhi nor any Congress leads would attend the discussions in England. Civil disobedience would continue.

Gandhi remained in Yerwada Central Jail into the winter of 1930. The Round Table Conference gathered in London without him. He rededicated himself to his prison life and put aside all thoughts of the independence movement. Dwelling on political events from his jail quarters was a misuse of his time and energy. Instead, he kept to his strict schedule of spinning as well as rest, prayers, reading, translation work, and letter writing. Most of these letters were to his ashramites, advising them on how to achieve their best, most spiritually whole selves. Gandhi was more focused than ever on the lessons of his favorite text. "I run to mother Gita, and to this day she has never failed to comfort me," he advised his nephew in November.

Under guidelines imposed by the prison commandant, Gandhi could not write to his fellow inmates—not even to his own son, Manilal, who was serving a year's sentence of hard labor for his actions at Dharasana. Instead, Gandhi communicated his good

wishes to his son through Manilal's wife, Sushila. According to Sushila's letters, Manilal had lost forty pounds while in jail, although he had largely recovered from the cracked skull and other wounds inflicted on him during the Dharasana raid. Gandhi reassured her that Manilal would endure. "God has given him the strength to live in all circumstances," he comforted her. "Moreover, he is simple at heart and so God always protects him."

Across India, the cycle of resistance and repression continued. The violence against his people pained Gandhi. But he believed that their moral and spiritual powers were growing with each day they endured the sticks and blows of the Raj.

Throughout every province of India, people were making that effort. With more strikes. More demonstrations. More boycotts. More violations of the salt laws. More bonfires of British cloth. More refusals to pay taxes of every kind. More arrests. More imprisonments. Lord Irwin informed the British cabinet that four provinces of India, whose population numbered almost one-third of the country's 320 million, might have to be placed under martial law or risk complete chaos. His forces struck back against the independence movement with brutality.

The repression did not escape notice at home. Noted British foreign correspondent Henry Brailsford finished a tour of India during the upheaval and published a damning article in the *Manchester Guardian* about what he witnessed. He described an attack on Calcutta University students who had heckled the police from the balcony of their classroom. Under the command of a British officer, the police "invaded the classroom and beat the students indiscriminately as they sat at their desks, till the walls were spattered with blood." Brailsford also told of an Indian lawyer turned activist who was shot at close range in the arm by police after giving a speech. The injured arm had to be amputated. Also in the article was the story of Gujarati peasants who had their land, buffalo, and even tools confiscated because they refused to pay a small tax. In story after story, Brailsford recounted beatings so vicious that "whole bodies were covered with marks," and described prisoners being kept in open-roofed iron cages like animals in a zoo.

By the end of 1930, Lord Irwin and the British government had lost the war of public opinion. This was made starkly clear when the popular American magazine *Time* chose Gandhi to be their Man of the Year. Once critical of his salt campaign, the publication had come to recognize his genius. "Curiously," *Time*'s editors explained, "it was in a jail that the year's end found the little half-naked brown man whose 1930 mark on world history will undoubtedly loom largest of all . . . It was in March that he marched to the sea to defy Britain's salt tax as some New Englanders once defied a British tea tax."

In January 1931, the two-month-long Round Table Conference in London came to a close. Without the leading figure in Indian politics or any Congress members on hand for the negotiations, they never had much of a chance of bringing about meaningful change. Beyond a vague construct of a future federal government that shared power between Britain and Indian legislators, its only real outcome was to highlight the huge challenge of building a state in which the two most populous religious groups, Hindus and Muslims, could not find common ground.

Afterward, the British prime minister Ramsay MacDonald publicly stated that he looked forward to "further negotiations" to settle on an Indian constitution. Privately, he pushed Irwin to launch talks again with Gandhi to finally end the civil disobedience campaign and to involve him directly in future talks. Agreeing with MacDonald that this was the only path forward, Irwin ordered the release of Gandhi and the other Congress leaders from prison.

At 11:00 p.m. on January 26, 1931, Gandhi emerged from Yerwada Central Jail. Sarojini Naidu was released at the same time, and the two were shuttled by car to nearby Chinchwad train station. When asked by a reporter on the platform if he had a message for the Indian people, Gandhi replied, "I have come out of jail with an absolutely open mind, unfettered by enmity, unbiased in argument, and prepared to study the whole situation." Then he and Naidu boarded the express to Bombay.

Chapter 15

Gandhi was welcomed at the Maidan in Bombay by crowds numbering over 200,000. Such was people's excitement to be near the Mahatma that there was a risk of a stampede and he had to abandon his speech, delivering his terms for peace. Instead, he spoke to the press. If the British wanted to so much as open discussions on ending the civil disobedience campaign, they had to do three things first: (1) release all satyagraha prisoners; (2) withdraw the stack of oppressive ordinances such as press censorship and limits on assemblies; and (3) acknowledge the right of Indians to picket foreign cloth and liquor shops.

As for his views on past negotiations and any future ones with the Raj in the matter of constitutional reform, Gandhi said, "I want the substance of independence—no shadow." He would only consider attending a Second Round Table Conference if there was some advancement on the eleven points of reform that he had demanded of the viceroy before the Salt March began. These included abolishing the salt tax, cuts in land taxes, restrictions on the police, and reductions in the military and civil spending that allowed the Raj to lord it over the Indian people.

From Bombay, Gandhi traveled to Allahabad to meet with other Congress leaders, including Jawaharlal Nehru and Sarojini Naidu. Again the crowds were so huge that Gandhi had to slip surreptitiously into and out of train stations to avoid the heaving masses of supporters. Throughout India, the civil resistance continued, and so too did the violent repression, including a lathi charge against a peaceful march of women and girls in Gujarat. While he was in Allahabad, Gandhi sent a letter to Irwin, asking for an inquiry into recent police brutalities. With such a sign of goodwill, Gandhi said, he would be much more open to meeting. The viceroy replied that an inquiry would do no good.

In the midst of this back-and-forth, Gandhi visited Motilal Nehru, who was gravely ill and on his deathbed. "I am going soon, Mahatmaji," Motilal told him. "I shall not be here to see swaraj. But I know you have won it and will soon have it." On February 6, while traveling to Lucknow for treatment for his illness, Motilal died. Gandhi was grief-stricken. He felt as if he had lost a member of his own family. Nehru's body was returned to Allahabad draped in the Congress flag. A funeral pyre was built on the banks where the Ganges and Jumna rivers met. Gandhi laid a piece of sandalwood on the still face of his old comrade in the fight against the British. More wood was piled onto the body by others, then Jawaharlal extended a burning torch toward his father's pyre. Cries of "Pandit Motilal Nehru ki jai!" rose into the sky. After the funeral, Gandhi delivered a message to the Indian people. "Let us deserve this hero's sacrifice by each sacrificing, if not all, at least enough to attain freedom, which he was yearning after and which is within easy grasp now."

The next day, Sapru and Jayakar, the moderate politicians who had tried to negotiate a settlement that previous summer and who both had attended the Round Table Conference in London, came to Allahabad. Again they urged Gandhi to seek a compromise with the viceroy to bring an end to the civil disobedience movement. The two moderates believed that the "bare outline" of a constitutional scheme created in London could be brought to fruition. The Congress needed only to end its campaign and join negotiations. It was these pleadings, but more his longtime friend's death, that convinced Gandhi to pursue talks. Motilal Nehru had always been a champion of independence. At times, he risked arrest, but he also understood there were moments for negotiation and openhearted talks. Gandhi now followed the latter.

On February 14, he wrote again to New Delhi. "I would like to meet not so much the viceroy of India as the man in you," Gandhi said. The response came quickly. Lord Irwin invited Gandhi to meet him at Viceroy's House the following Tuesday, February 17. At 2:15 p.m. on the appointed day, a dark-green car rolled around the manicured courtyard in front of Viceroy's House. When Gandhi emerged from the back of the car, red-coated servants hurried out to welcome him, and he was aided up the long marble stairs to the main hall.

Even though Gandhi was fifteen minutes early for the appointed meeting, Irwin's private secretary, George Cunningham, was ready and waiting to receive him. Cunningham escorted him to the viceroy's study and then left to inform "His Excellency" of the arrival. Irwin was in his private apartment, expectant. His tenure as viceroy was drawing to a close, and in mid-April he would be leaving India for England. He had spent the past week celebrating the completion of India's new capital.

One of the grandest events was the unveiling of the four ornamental "Dominion Columns" that stood on the square before the domed Imperial Secretariat Building. Carved from red sandstone, they rose forty-one feet above the surrounding lawns, fountains, and pools. The columns were gifts from the four key self-governing countries within the British Commonwealth: Canada, Australia, South Africa, and New Zealand. Irwin, in his capacity as viceroy, led the processional from the palace to the columns for the unveiling. Wearing a scarlet uniform and plumed helmet, he rode in an open-top carriage drawn by six horses. A thirty-one-gun salute, a blare of trumpets, and Britain's anthem "God Save the King" preceded his speech about the empire's friendship with India. "Devoutly let us pray," he said, "that these four pillars of fellowship now given to India may forever symbolize such association."

But before he could depart India in good conscience, Irwin had one last piece of business: securing a settlement with Gandhi. He knew he was taking a risk—welcoming the leader of a movement that did not recognize the king's right to rule India. Gandhi had called the British Raj "satanic" and had fostered a rebellion—nonviolent though it mostly was—that had caused chaos throughout the country.

In Westminster, Conservatives, led by the irascible Winston Churchill, strongly argued against Irwin negotiating with Gandhi. "Gandhism and all it stands for will, sooner or later, have to be grappled with and finally crushed. It is no use trying to satisfy a tiger by feeding him with cat's meat."

Despite this condemnation, Irwin sensed that a settlement could be reached between Gandhi and himself. In a January 17 speech, he made overtures about opening talks by first paying tribute to the independence leader: "No one can fail to recognize the spiritual force which impels Mr. Gandhi to count no sacrifice too great in the cause, as he believes, of the India that he loves." And despite Gandhi's heated rhetoric against the British Raj, Irwin was confident that he was a master of political calculation who would know a good deal when it was presented to him. Furthermore, Irwin believed that he understood Gandhi—thanks in no small part to a conversation he had had with Charles Freer Andrews.

In his memoir, Irwin recounted this insight: "Constitutional reform was important and necessary for the development of India's personality and self-respect; but what really mattered to Gandhi were the things that affect the daily lives of the millions of his fellow countrymen—salt, opium, cottage industries, and the like . . . He was the natural knight-errant, fighting always the battle of the weak against suffering and what he judged injustice." Given this understanding, Irwin knew he had a starting point for a settlement.

As for his critics, they might accuse Irwin of softness and of "betrayal of the empire," but that was just political point-scoring and denial of the realities of what was happening in India. Irwin knew his history. He knew that force alone could not stem the tide of India's political awakening without sacrificing the very ideals of his own nation's democracy. "No Englishman can," he later stated, "without being false to his own history, and in recent years to his own pledges, take objection to pursuit by others of their own political liberty."

Once informed of Gandhi's arrival, Irwin left his private apartment and went to his study, where he found his guest already seated. He greeted him warmly, the door closed, and the two were left alone for the next four hours to have a heart-to-heart talk. It was a meeting of equals, and nothing like it had ever occurred between the British and an Indian leader since the East India Company first landed in the Indian subcontinent in 1608.

Like most negotiations, there were fits and starts, blustery proposals and supposed deadlocks. The two were never going to come to terms on the issue of Indian independence. That was a discussion for the next Round Table Conference. They were there to put in place an agreement, if they could, that would see the Indian National Congress agree to take part in the next Round

Table in London and satisfy Gandhi's list of demands, convincing him to call off the civil disobedience campaign. No small task.

On the first day, Gandhi and Lord Irwin focused on the overall political situation and the future of India. Initially, the two were rather cautious of each other, and their conversation was halting. After a couple of hours, they grew more comfortable with each other and launched into the finer points of negotiation. What to do about the salt tax? What of other taxes? How to handle political prisoners? What about lands and other property confiscated by the Raj? What limits would there be on the picketing and boycotting of goods? To what degree would there be inquiries into police misconduct?

After the first meeting with Irwin, Gandhi told an associate, "He seemed to be a good man with good intentions." Gandhi was impressed by Irwin's openness and by how moved Irwin had been by the courage and sacrifices of the satyagraha volunteers. For his part, Irwin was impressed by Gandhi's directness and his agile mind.

Shortly before dusk, Irwin warmly wished Gandhi a good night, and Gandhi did the same. They planned to meet again the next day. The car that had brought Gandhi was waiting in the courtyard, and a herd of reporters pressed forward to ask him how the discussion had gone. Gandhi ducked the question. He and the viceroy had agreed to keep their conversations private. The press guessed anyway: "The Viceroy and Mr. Gandhi—Four Hours' Talk—Further

Meeting," declared *The Times* of London. "Optimism Grows in India" was the headline in the *New York Times*. "Bright Hopes of Early Settlement" came the banner of the *Times of India*, enthusiastic about the progress.

Not everybody was pleased with the developments. Jawaharlal Nehru believed they should not bother with any negotiations that did not bring immediate Indian independence. Many in the Congress party agreed with him. On the British side, nobody was more scathing than Churchill, who let loose a tirade against Lord Irwin and Gandhi: "In my opinion we ought to dissociate ourselves in the most public and formal manner from any complicity in the weak, wrong-headed, and most unfortunate administration of India . . . It was alarming and also nauseating to see Mr. Gandhi, a one-time Inner Temple lawyer, who had now become a seditious saint of a type well known in the East, striding half-naked up the steps of the Viceregal Palace, while he was still organizing and conducting a defiant campaign of civil disobedience, to parley on equal terms with the representative of the King-Emperor."

But despite news headlines and pushback from some on both sides, any future deal rested on Gandhi and Lord Irwin. On Wednesday, February 18, they met again. A chilly spell had fallen over New Delhi, and a fire was lit in Irwin's study. Comforted by its warm glow, they talked again for several hours, each taking notes on the other's positions and where agreement could be reached. At one point, Irwin offered his guest tea. Gandhi accepted and, after his cup was poured, drew a folded paper from his shawl. Inside it

was some salt. "I will put some of this salt into my tea to remind us of the famous Boston Tea Party," Gandhi said, always keen for a little symbolism. The two men laughed and continued their discussion until the early evening. They reached an impasse over the scope of the next Round Table talks, what to do about the salt tax, and the future of any investigations into police misconduct. Both sides feared the other would not move their starting positions.

"It is all hanging up in the clouds," Gandhi told the press upon emerging from the palace. He offered nothing else. The next day, he returned for a half hour. There were, again, few advancements. The two decided to suspend the talks, each man wanting to consult with his own team. A week went by. Gandhi was staying in a comfortable bungalow in Old Delhi, overlooking the Jumna River. The house was owned by Dr. Mukhtar Ansari, a noted physician and nationalist, who had opened his home for Gandhi to stay during the talks. There Gandhi spun, prayed, met with Congress leaders, and ruminated over the possible deal that might be struck. Irwin convened with his own advisers, corresponded with London, attended farewell parties, and prepared for his family's return to England.

On Friday, February 27, Gandhi and Lord Irwin began what would turn into six straight days of negotiations.

In all his political career, Irwin had never negotiated with a more persistent, mercurial, wily, and strange individual as Mohandas Karamchand Gandhi. But when one of Irwin's secretaries spoke of how "tiresome" Gandhi was, Irwin's response was "A lot of people found our Lord Jesus tiresome." Gandhi often waxed long-windedly on issues such as an official inquiry into police misconduct only to surrender his position as soon as Lord Irwin agreed with him that he had the right to *make* such requests but that they were impossible to execute in practice. Seemingly, Gandhi was satisfied with having won the moral argument. On other occasions, Gandhi wouldn't relinquish what seemed to Irwin a tiny matter.

Steadily, they knocked out draft after draft of an agreement. Gandhi and several other Congress members would attend the next Round Table to formulate the constitutional future of India. The civil disobedience campaign would be suspended. The viceroy agreed to allow continued picketing of liquor and British goods stores so long as protesters were restrained and peaceful. Imprisoned satyagrahis would go free, and repressive ordinances against civil liberties would be lifted. As for salt, peasants would be allowed to harvest salt without paying a tax if it was for personal consumption. The salt tax would otherwise remain intact. Investigations into police misconduct would be limited; seized lands that had already been sold would not be returned; and there would be no relief from the death penalty for several individuals who had committed terrorist acts in the name of Indian freedom. Independence from Britain or dominion status were not addressed.

Finally, on March 5, the two signed what would become known as the Gandhi-Irwin Pact in one of Viceroy House's grand halls. Afterward, they had tea, joked about how Churchill had called Gandhi a "half-naked fakir," and celebrated their hard-won negotiations. As Gandhi was preparing to leave that night, Irwin stopped him. He had forgotten his shawl. Smiling, Irwin said, "Gandhi, you haven't so much on, you know, that you can afford to leave this behind."

"The Viceroy's Triumph" was the banner headline in *The Times* of London. The article read, "Lord Irwin will end his term of office with such a victory as has seldom been vouchsafed to a Viceroy." Irwin's own government heralded his statesmanship and dealmaking too. The *Times of India* remarked, "His concessions will not be found to have been made at too great a price," summarizing the popular sentiment that the viceroy had achieved better terms than Gandhi had given.

Meanwhile, Gandhi suffered barbs from many of his own supporters that Irwin had gotten the better of him, that he had all but surrendered to the British. The settlement lacked any guarantees of future independence. Not even the salt tax had been fully eliminated. The British still ruled over India. Gandhi tried to allay the concerns of the Indian press and his fellow Congress leaders. He had spared India further pain that a breakdown in talks would have "intensified a hundredfold." Purna swaraj was still his aim, he said. The work must continue to reach that goal, but for now, that would come, hopefully, by "patient negotiation, consultation, and conference."

Shortly after the talks concluded, Gandhi left for Ahmedabad by third-class carriage, beginning a cross-country tour by train. Enormous crowds greeted him at every station. He made it clear that the struggle continued and that "there can be no question of victory without reaching the goal" of complete independence.

American journalist William Shirer, who reported on the talks from New Delhi, wrote: "For the first time since the British took away India from the Indians, they had been forced, as Churchill bitterly complained, to deal with an Indian leader as an equal. For the first time the British acknowledged that Gandhi represented the demand of most of the Indians for self-government . . . They could no longer be permanently suppressed, nor their goals of Indian independence for very much longer denied. From now on it was a question not of whether the British were willing to grant independence to India, but of *how* and *when*."

The Salt March, and the widespread civil disobedience campaign that it inspired, were over. Talks in London were the next step. Freedom for India remained unwon, but the country, its people, and the British Raj were forever changed. That is what Gandhi gained from his campaign that ended with the pact signed in New Delhi. Only time would reveal its genius. Henry Polak, a British-born lawyer who had supported Gandhi in South Africa, wrote, "What, then, had Indians won by this year of nonviolent revolt? They had freed their own minds. They had won independence in their hearts." Beyond advancing India's fight for freedom, Gandhi and his fellow salt thieves gave the world a blueprint on how to achieve political change not by the fist, the sword, the gun, or the bomb but rather through fearless, peaceful protest.

Gandhi awakened the world to the plight of his compatriots and their suffering under the heel of the British Raj. More important, he empowered millions of Indians to act, nonviolently, against that regime, and he awakened in them the possibility of self-determination and freedom. Dr. Aloo Jehan Dastur was one of those millions. When the campaign began, in March 1930, she was a student at Bombay University on the verge of graduation. She dropped out of college to participate in marches and to harvest illegal salt. In an interview later in life, she explained succinctly the impact of the salt movement: "Gandhi showed what the Indian was made of, both man and woman. He restored to us Indians our erect posture. He made us look any foreigner in the face. He made us shed our fear of the lathi, the prison house, even the bullet. This was no mean achievement, and, since this was done, it was evident that freedom could not be delayed much longer. The Indian by 1930 had, so to say, found his soul."

Chapter 16

Before Lord Irwin left India on April 18, 1931, his term as viceroy at an end, a state ball was given in his honor. "It was a wonderful warm evening," one of the attendees remembered. "With the background of Lutyens's fountains, and the lights of Imperial Delhi and the gay uniforms of the men, and the long flowing dresses of the women, and the distant music of the band, it seemed as if old Versailles had come to life . . . We enjoy the great gala nights of Viceregal hospitality all the more because we wonder uneasily how much longer they will continue." It would be sixteen years before they did end and the Indian people obtained their independence.

From the moment Lord Irwin left India, he had little influence over the future of India. A year away from politics and time on his rural estate awaited him in England. The peace deal with Gandhi secured his reputation for steadfast, wise leadership. He rejoined the government in 1932 as president of the Board of Education and a member of Prime Minister Ramsay MacDonald's cabinet. Two years later, he became Viscount Halifax, inheriting the title upon his father's death.

As Lord Halifax, his rise would continue, first as secretary of state for war, then as Leader of the House of Lords, then as foreign secretary under Neville Chamberlain in the run-up to World War II. He took a balanced position on Hitler's first aggression, pushing for negotiation with Germany rather than war, while simultaneously pressing for the rearmament of England if things went bad. With Germany's annexation of Austria and its invasion of Poland, things went very bad, very quickly.

In 1940, with the fall of Chamberlain's government, there was tremendous support from the king to many in Parliament for Lord Halifax to become the British prime minister during the war set to rage throughout Europe. Instead of seizing his chance, he stepped back to allow Winston Churchill to take the reins of government. Lord Halifax believed his former tormentor during his time as viceroy of India would provide the kind of energetic, do-or-die leadership necessary in the fight against the Nazis. History would prove Lord Halifax right, much as it would his belief that independence was inevitable for India.

He served as ambassador to the United States throughout WWII, then finally retired from government soon afterward. In his memoirs, Irwin spoke plainly about his experiences with Gandhi. Many of them tested his patience, but he was also clear on his respect for the man, saying, "this most remarkable human figure was larger than any of the attempts made to paint his portrait."

At midday, on August 29, 1931, the SS *Rajputana* steamed out of Bombay with Gandhi aboard. It was bringing him to the constitutional negotiations of the Second Round Table Conference in London, where he would represent the Indian National Congress. Accompanying Gandhi on the voyage were Sarojini Naidu; Gandhi's youngest son, Devadas; and three of his ashramites. En route, Gandhi spoke to a Reuters correspondent and described the future he hoped for his homeland: "I shall work for an India in which the poorest shall feel that it is their country in whose making they have an effective voice; an India in which there shall be no high class or low class of people; an India in which all communities shall live in harmony."

While in London, Gandhi did not take a room in a grand hotel, nor even one close to St. James's Palace, where the conference was taking place. Instead, he stayed at Kingsley Hall, a building run by Quakers that served the needy in the heart of London's impoverished East End. Gandhi's room resembled a closet and had a stone floor and bare, cracked walls. He liked to sit on the rooftop to work his charka, and in the mornings he walked through the local slums, greeting and smiling at his neighbors.

If the Salt March made Gandhi famous around the world, the time he spent in London endeared him to it. The press trailed him everywhere he went, snapping photographs of him in his familiar attire of khadi and sandals. He looked so out of place—and yet so at ease. On his first day in London, he gave a radio interview to the Columbia Broadcasting Service in which he appealed "to the conscience of the world to come to the rescue of a people dying for regaining its liberty." This was the first time millions in the United States had heard his voice, and his message.

As usual, Gandhi kept a frenzied schedule. When not at the Round Table discussions, he was sitting down with reporters, touring working-class districts, reuniting with old friends, visiting members of Parliament, and trading quips with celebrities like Charlie Chaplin. He even had afternoon tea with King George V and Queen Mary at Buckingham Palace.

One day, he met with Webb Miller and chided the American reporter for not visiting him when he was in India. Miller responded that Gandhi had been in jail. "So I was," Gandhi replied. "I spend a good deal of my time in jails." The two then spoke about the influence American writer Henry David Thoreau had had on Gandhi, and the influence Hindu literature had had on Thoreau—and how such was the eternal and international trade in ideas.

Unfortunately, regarding the immediate freedom he sought for his people, Gandhi had little influence on the Round Table discussions. He was outmaneuvered by the British, who followed their old playbook strategy of divide and conquer. They were pushing for separate electorates among communal groups, such as Muslims, Untouchables, Sikhs, Hindus, and various princely states. As the British intended, this threw the Round Table Conference into disarray, hobbling any efforts to advance the key issue in Gandhi's mind: the transfer of power.

Politically, the Second Round Table Conference accomplished as much as the first had done. Nothing. An embittered Gandhi returned to India on December 28, 1931, and found that the new viceroy, Lord Willingdon, was not only stalling over fulfilling the obligations promised under the pact with Irwin but was also imposing renewed repressive measures against Congress. Jawaharlal Nehru had already been arrested. When Gandhi promised to restart a civil disobedience campaign, he was arrested as well.

Fifteen more years would pass before the Indian people won complete independence from Britain. Gandhi spent many of them in jail. There were more widespread resistance campaigns, including strikes, marches, and boycotts. The Raj arrested tens of thousands and instituted severe repressions over and over again. A string of viceroys filed through the palace, none with the vision of Lord Irwin. Despite some significant efforts at constitutional reform, including the 1935 Government of India Act that allowed provincial elections, the independence movement continued. Divisions festered between communities, in part because of this reform, and there were periodic outbreaks of violence between Hindus and Muslims. Satyagrahis acted courageously against this divide as well as against the government. Throughout, Gandhi championed nonviolence, even in the darkest of moments. In 1944, Kasturba Gandhi, his wife of sixty years, passed away in a detention camp, as did Gandhi's personal secretary, Mahadev Desai. While in jail, Gandhi went on several hunger strikes that almost killed him.

At last, on August 15, 1947, India had its freedom. Devastated after World War II, Britain could no longer fund or hold on to an empire whose people strained to be released from its grasp. Furthermore, America, Britain's ally in the war, pressed for the disassembling of the British Empire, especially in India. On the eve of India's independence, Jawaharlal Nehru addressed the Constituent Assembly of India in New Delhi's Parliament House. His words are considered one of the finest speeches of the twentieth century. He began:

> *Long years ago, we made a tryst with destiny, and now the time comes when we shall redeem our pledge . . . At the stroke of the midnight hour, when the world sleeps, India will awake to life and freedom. A moment comes, which comes but rarely in history, when we step out from the old to the new, when an age ends, and when the soul of a nation, long suppressed, finds utterance. It is fitting that at this solemn moment we take the pledge of dedication to the service of India and her people and to the still larger cause of humanity.*

Supported by Gandhi, whom he called "The Father of Our Nation," Nehru was elected India's first prime minister, a position he served in for eighteen years. He shaped India's democratic government and led its economy, education system, social practices, and foreign policy into the modern age. He became renowned as a great statesman.

But the independence that India won was not the independence that Gandhi wanted. The Muslim League led by Muhammad Ali Jinnah had demanded its own state (or at least a decentralized national government) after elections the decade before had solidified Congress's hold in the majority of provinces. As Jinnah stated, the Muslim League did not want to "get rid of the present slavery under the British and [suffer a] future of Caste Hindu domination." Under negotiations led by Lord Mountbatten, the last viceroy of India, the northwestern and northeastern flanks of the British Raj (both of which contained Muslim majorities) were cleaved off to create Pakistan. Most of the rest of the subcontinent would become the Republic of India. This British division of territories, known as "Partition," led to huge migrations of Hindu and Muslim refugees, approximately fifteen million in number. It was also the cause of terrible outbreaks of violence. Close to a million people died in ugly riots and massacres between the two sides.

By the sheer force of his will, Gandhi stepped in and stopped the bloodshed. He traveled about the partitioned country, often at the risk of being swept away in the mobs, preaching calm and forgiveness. He also went on what he called his "greatest fast," which lasted until peace was restored in mid-January 1948. At seventy-eight years old, he was tempting death with every such physical trial.

On January 30, 1948, Gandhi was in New Delhi, at Birla House, where he had been staying throughout his hunger strike. As usual, he met with a host of visitors throughout the day, planning the future of India and discussing how to prevent further communal violence. At 5:15 p.m., he left the house and headed to the garden for a prayer meeting. He supported himself with a hand on the shoulders of two of his grand-nieces, Abha and Manu.

As Gandhi stepped up to the raised lawn where he would preach, a man in a khaki shirt and blue trousers approached him. The man knocked Abha Gandhi aside, drew a pistol, and fired three times at the Mahatma. All three bullets struck their target, and Gandhi collapsed to the ground, blood mushrooming out onto the woolen shawl draped across his chest. He died soon afterward. The surrounding crowd grabbed the gunman, a militant Hindu nationalist called Nathuram Godse, who believed that Gandhi was betraying his own faith by urging reconciliation with Muslims.

It was an end that Gandhi had long expected, and he had mastered his fear of it many years before. Tragic though his assassination was—and immense the outpouring of grief throughout the world that followed—he died because he sought peace. Sarojini Naidu attended his funeral. As the flames transmuted the remains of his body, the gathered masses on the banks of the Jumna River cried out, "The Mahatma has become eternal." Afterward, Naidu made an eloquent speech that was broadcast on All India Radio, bringing comfort to millions of mourners.

> *The time is over for beating of breasts and tearing of hair. The time is here and now when we stand up and say, "We take up the challenge" to those who defied Mahatma Gandhi. We are his living symbols. We are his soldiers. We are the carriers*

> *of his banner before an embattled world. Our banner is truth. Our shield is nonviolence. Our sword is a sword of the spirit that conquers without blood. Let the peoples of India rise up and wipe their tears, rise up and still their sobs, rise up and be full of hope and full of cheer.*

Naidu committed the rest of her life to fulfilling the promise of her speech. Appointed governor of the United Provinces in northern India, she was the country's first woman to hold high office. She died of a heart attack while working at her desk in March 1949, the Nightingale of India silent too soon.

Manilal Gandhi was in Durban, South Africa, buying fruit and vegetables in the market when he learned of his father's assassination. "Complete blankness seems to have seized me," he recalled. Over the past few months, Gandhi had sent letters to his son expressing how proud he was of him, both for his dedication to the weekly paper and to the nonviolence struggle, and even to his recent experiments with his diet. Now he was gone, and Manilal could not even attend the funeral. "My grief," he said, "was drowned in the ocean of grief of the whole world." Even then he had to share his father with so many others.

Manilal had returned to South Africa in 1931, soon after being released from prison. As before, he lived at the Phoenix Settlement, served as publisher of the *Indian Opinion*, and campaigned

inexhaustibly for the equal rights of Indians in South Africa. He and Sushila had two more children, and the family of five followed the ascetic ways of the ashram that Gandhi had set out when he founded the farm in 1904.

On the day India obtained its independence, Manilal rose early and, with several thousand other Indians, gathered on a beach before dawn. At 6:00 a.m., as the sun hinted on the horizon and a splendid morning breeze blew, he raised the new flag of India. "It was truly a sight for the gods to see," he later wrote. Nonetheless, like his father, Manilal was grief-stricken over the clashes between Muslims and Hindus as well as the partitioning of the country.

Manilal Gandhi continued to fight racial discrimination in South Africa, both for Indians and for Black people. He went on hunger strikes and spent more time in prison. For the rest of his life, he carried the scars from the lathi blows he had received at Dharasana. He considered his efforts there, at "that great moment in our history," to be some of the finest of a life spent in nonviolent resistance.

Almost one hundred years have passed since Mahatma Gandhi and his band of seventy-eight marchers first set out from the Satyagraha Ashram in Ahmedabad. Their actions became legend in India. The Salt March is taught in schools, memorialized in film, and commemorated in monuments and statues. Anniversaries of the march typically attract thousands of pilgrims who retrace the route from the Satyagraha Ashram to Dandi.

As the Indian social reformer Gopal Krishna Gokhale said,

Gandhi had that rare ability to "mold heroes out of common clay." These heroes helped free India from the British Empire. The campaign empowered Indians across the subcontinent to cast away their fear of the British Raj, to embrace their collective strength as a people, and to seek independence.

Epilogue

"I can say without arrogance, and in all humility," Gandhi once wrote, "that my message and methods are in essence meant for the entire world." As a legacy, his achievements would be significant enough. But they were only the starting point.

Martin Luther King, Jr., was very clear on who was the inspiration for his methods when fighting for equal rights for Black Americans through sit-ins, freedom rides, and marches on Washington, DC. While a graduate seminary student in Philadelphia, Dr. King was electrified by Gandhi's philosophy. He read everything he could find on the Indian resistance leader. In his first book, *Stride Toward Freedom*, Dr. King wrote,

> *Gandhi was probably the first person in history to lift the love ethic of Jesus above mere interaction between individuals to a powerful and effective social force on a large scale . . . I came to feel that this was the only morally and practically sound method open to oppressed people in their struggle for freedom . . . this principle became the guiding light of our movement. Christ furnished the spirit and motivation and Gandhi furnished the method.*

In 1958, South African prime minister Hendrik Verwoerd said of his government, "Our motto is to maintain white supremacy for all time." Starting with Black activists like Albert Lutuli, who considered himself a "disciple of Gandhi," nonviolent action proved instrumental in ending the country's ingrained laws of apartheid and leading Nelson Mandela to become South Africa's first Black president in 1994.

Gandhi also influenced other anticolonial campaigns in Africa, including in Kenya, Zambia, Tanzania, Ghana, and Botswana—all of which gained their independence between 1957 and 1966.

And many, many more followed the path of nonviolence to effect political change: The People Power movement in the Philippines led by Corazon Aquino, the widow of an assassinated opposition leader. The overthrow of Chilean dictator Augusto Pinochet. The casting off of the chains of the Soviet Union in Poland, Czechoslovakia, and across Eastern Europe. The Rose Revolution in Georgia, the Orange Revolution in Ukraine, the Cedar Revolution in Lebanon, the Saffron Revolution in Myanmar, the Bulldozer Revolution in Yugoslavia . . . Czech playwright turned independence leader Václav Havel wrote that those fighting an authoritarian regime did not need "soldiers of its own." Instead, they had as their source of strength, "everyone who is living with the lie and who may be struck at any moment by the force of truth." He was echoing Gandhi with these words.

The truth is that Mohandas Karamchand Gandhi was no saint.

He was human, an often harsh, unyielding father and husband. He could be obsessive and judgmental in his views on everything from celibacy, medicine, and diet, to the perils of the modern age. As Jawaharlal Nehru once said of him, Gandhi was "a great man, but he had his weaknesses, his moods, and his failings. We Hindus have a tendency to turn anyone we see as great into a god. But Gandhi was much too human and complex to be one." Gandhi might have been more human than saint, but the method of nonviolent resistance seen in the Salt March still resonates today.

History has proven that the Mahatma's methods were practical too. According to one academic study, whose authors reviewed 323 campaigns to bring about significant political change between 1900 and 2006, nonviolent methods were twice as likely as violent ones to succeed.

Not every such movement achieved its end. Among the highest-profile failures were the student-led demonstrations in 1989 China. Tens of thousands of young Chinese people marched on Tiananmen Square in the heart of Beijing, calling for democracy. The movement was gathering momentum when the Communist Party declared martial law and moved on the protesters, opening fire and killing thousands. At one point, a lone man with a shopping bag in each hand stopped a line of advancing tanks, creating an iconic image of peaceful resistance. But his heroic act, and many others like it, were not enough to usher in change, particularly since the Chinese government was shamelessly willing to use deadly force on its own citizens and to endure the backlash from the international community afterward.

Even so, nonviolent resistance movements over the past century have been extremely effective. Women's rights, LGBTQIA+ rights, Native American rights—their movements' leaders in the United States spearheaded nonviolent political protests inspired by Gandhi's concept of satyagraha to successfully obtain their goals. Almost daily in America and across the world, people take to the streets to march for what they believe and to have their voices heard.

BIBLIOGRAPHY

Oral History, Centre of South Asian Studies, University of Cambridge

Ali, A; Batilwala, S.; Captain, G.; Dastur, A.; Deo, S.; Deogirikar, T. R.; Desai, K.; Dhurandhar, B. R.; Harkare, D. R.; Joshi, C.; Kabadi, S.; Krishna, R.; Lal, B. C.; Lal, S.; Mehta, H.; Nair, C. K.; Narayanswami, C. K.; Qureshi, G; Sahni, J. N.

Primary Source Material

Phatak, N. R., ed. *Mahatma Gandhi: Source Material for a History of the Freedom Movement in India*, vol. 3, part 1: *1915–1922*. Bombay Directorate of Printing & Stationery, 1965.

___. *Mahatma Gandhi: Source Material for a History of the Freedom Movement in India*, vol. 3, part 2: *1922–1929*. Bombay Directorate of Printing & Stationery, 1968.

___. *Mahatma Gandhi: Source Material for a History of the Freedom Movement in India*, vol. 3, part 3: *1929–1931*. Bombay Directorate of Printing & Stationery, 1969.

The Collected Works of Mahatma Gandhi. Ahmedabad: Ministry of Information and Broadcasting, 1965.

Selected Works of Jawaharlal Nehru, vol. 4. New Delhi: Orient Longman, 1972.

Contemporaneous Periodicals

Bombay Chronicle
Daily Telegraph
Indian Opinion

Le Journal
Le Petit Parisien
Manchester Guardian
Times (London)
Times of India
Young India

Books

Ackerman, Peter, and Jack DuVall. *A Force More Powerful: A Century of Nonviolent Conflict*. New York: St. Martin's Press, 2000.

Amin, Shahid. *Event, Metaphor, Memory: Chauri Chaura 1922–1992*. Berkeley: University of California Press, 1995.

Ashe, Geoffrey. *Gandhi*. New York: Stein & Day, 1972.

Banerjea, Pramathanath. *A History of Indian Taxation*. London: Macmillan and Co., 1930.

Basu, Aparna. *Women in Satyagraha*. New Delhi: Ministry of Information and Broadcasting, 2018.

Bernays, Robert. *Naked Fakir*. London: Victor Gollancz, 1931.

Bolton, Glorney. *The Tragedy of Gandhi*. London: George Allen & Unwin, 1934.

Bose, Subhas Chandra. *The Indian Struggle, 1920–1934*. London: Wishart & Company, 1935.

Brown, Judith. *Gandhi and Civil Disobedience: The Mahatma in Indian Politics, 1928–1934*. Cambridge University Press, 2008.

Chandiwala, Brijkrishna. *At the Feet of Bapu*. Ahmedabad: Navajivan Publishing House, 1954.

Chaudhary, Ramnarayan. *Bapu as I Saw Him*. Ahmedabad: Navajivan Publishing House, 1960.

Chenoweth, Erica, and Maria Stephan. *Why Civil Resistance Works: The Strategic Logic of Nonviolent Conflict*. New York: Columbia University Press, 2011.

Coatman, John. *Years of Destiny: India, 1926–1932*. London: Jonathan Cape, 1932.

Collins, Larry, and Dominque LaPiere. *Freedom at Midnight*. New York: Simon & Schuster, 1975.

Dalal, C. B. *Gandhi: 1915–1948: A Detailed Chronology*. New Delhi: Gandhi Peace Foundation, 1971.

Dalton, Dennis. *Mahatma Gandhi: Nonviolent Power in Action*. New York: Columbia University Press, 1995.

Dhawan, Gopinath. *The Political Philosophy of Mahatma Gandhi*. Ahmedabad: Navajivan Publishing House, 1946.

Dhupelia-Mesthrie, Uma. *Gandhi's Prisoner? The Life of Gandhi's Son Manilal*. South Africa: Kwela Books, 2004.

Dwarkadas, Kanji. *Gandhiji through My Diary Leaves, 1915–1948*. Vakil & Sons, 1950.

Farson, Negley. *The Way of a Transgressor*. New York: Literary Guild of America, 1936.

Fischer, Louis. *The Life of Mahatma Gandhi*. London: Jonathan Cape, 1957.

Gandhi, Arun, and Sunanda Gandhi, with Carol Lynn Yellin. *The Forgotten Woman: The Untold Story of Kastur Gandhi, Wife of Mahatma Gandhi*. Huntsville, AR: Ozark Mountain Publishers, 1998.

Gandhi, M. K. *From Yeravda Mandir: Ashram Observances*. Ahmedabad: Jivanji Desai, 1935.

Gandhi, Mohandas. *An Autobiography: The Story of My Experiments with Truth*. New York: Dover Publications, 1983.

Gopal, Sarvepalli. *The Viceroyalty of Lord Irwin, 1926–1931*. London: Oxford University Press, 1957.

Guha, Ramachandra. *Gandhi: The Years That Changed the World, 1914–1948*. New York: Vintage Books, 2019.

Gujarat Provincial Congress Committee. *The Black Regime at Dharasana: A Brief Survey of the Dharasana Raid*. Ahmedabad: Gujarat Provincial Congress Committee, 1930.

Hardiman, David. *Peasant Nationalists of Gujarat: Kheda District, 1917–1934*. New Delhi: Oxford University Press, 1981.

Hemingway, F. R. *Trichinopoly*. Madras: Madras Government Publications, 1907.

Ilahi, Shereen. "The Empire of Violence: Strategies of British Rule in India and Ireland in the Aftermath of the Great War." PhD diss., University of Texas at Austin, 2008.

Kripalani, J. B. *Gandhi: His Life and Thought*. New Delhi: Government of India, 1970.

Kurlansky, Mark. *Salt: A World History*. New York: Penguin Books, 2002.

Lelyveld, Joseph. *Great Soul: Mahatma Gandhi and His Struggle with India*. New York: Knopf, 2011.

McArthur, Brian. *Penguin Book of Twentieth Century Speeches*. London: Penguin Viking, 1992.

Mehta, Ved. *Mahatma Gandhi and His Apostles*. New York: Penguin Books, 1977.

Miller, Webb. *I Found No Peace: The Journal of a Foreign Correspondent*. New York: Simon & Schuster, 1936.

Mitra, Nripendra, ed. *The Indian Annual Register: January–June 1930*. Calcutta: Annual Register Office, 1931.

Molony, Charles. *A Book of South India*. London: Methuen & Company, 1926.

Morton, Eleanor. *The Women in Gandhi's Life*. New York: Dodd, Mead & Co, 1953.

Muzumdar, Haridas. *Gandhi the Apostle: His Trial and His Message*. Chicago: Universal Publishing Company, 1923.

___. *Gandhi Versus the Empire*. New York: Universal Publishing Company, 1932.

Nanda, B. R., ed. *Mahatma Gandhi, 125 Years*. New Delhi: Indian Council for Cultural Relations, 1995.

___. *The Nehrus: Motilal and Jawaharlal*. London: George Allen & Unwin, 1962.

Nayar, Sushila. *Mahatma Gandhi*, vol. 4: *Satyagraha at Work*. Ahmedabad: Navajivan Publishing House, 1995.

Nehru, Jawaharlal. *An Autobiography*. New Delhi: Oxford University Press, 1982.

___. *A Bunch of Old Letters*. Bombay: Asia Publishing House, 1960.

Paranjape, Makarand R., ed. *Sarojini Naidu: Selected Letters, 1890s–1940s*. New Delhi: Kali for Women, 1996.

Polak, Henry, H. N. Brailsford, and Lord Pethick-Lawrence. *Mahatma Gandhi*. London: Odhams Press, 1949.

Prasad, Rajendra. *At the Feet of Mahatma Gandhi*. Bombay: Hind Kitabs Publishers, 1955).

Reynolds, Reginald. *To Live in Mankind: A Quest for Gandhi*. London: Andre Deutsch, 1951.

Roberts, Adam, and Timothy Garton Ash, eds. *Civil Resistance and Power Politics: The Experience of Non-Violent Action from Gandhi to the Present*. London: Oxford University Press, 2009.

Roberts, Andrew. *"The Holy Fox": A Biography of Lord Halifax*. London: Weidenfeld & Nicolson, 1991.

Sharma, K. K., ed. *Perspectives on Sarojini Naidu*. Ghaziabad: Vimal Prakashan, 1989.

Sharp, Gene. *Gandhi Wields the Weapon of Moral Power*. Ahmedabad: Navajivan Publishing House, 1960.

Shirer, William L. *Gandhi: A Mem*oir. Calcutta: Rupa & Company, 1993.

Sitaramayya, B. Pattabhi. *History of the Indian National Congress*, vol. 1: *1885–1935*. Delhi: S. Chand & Co, 1969.

Slade, Madeline. *The Spirit's Pilgrimage*. New York: Coward-McCann, 1960.

Sudhir, Pillarisetti. "British Attitude to Indian Nationalism 1922–1935." PhD thesis, University of London, 1984.

Tendulkar, D. G. *Mahatma: Life of Mohandas Karamchand Gandhi*, vol. 3: *1930–1934*. New Delhi: Government of India, Ministry of Information and Broadcasting, 1961.

Tewari, Jyotsna. *Sabarmati to Dandi: Gandhi's Non Violent March and the Raj*. New Delhi: Rajpal Publications, 1995.

Tharoor, Shashi. *Inglorious Empire: What the British Did to India*. London: Scribe Publications, 2017).

The Earl of Halifax. *Fulness of Days*. London: Collins, 1957.

Wagner, Kim. *Amritsar 1919: An Empire of Fear and the Making of a Massacre*. Yale University Press, 2019.

Watson, Francis, ed. *Talking of Gandhiji: Four Programmes for Radio First Broadcast by the BBC*. New Delhi: Gandhi Smarak Nidhi, 1965.

Weber, Thomas. *On the Salt March: The Historiography of Gandhi's March to Dandi*. HarperCollins India, 1997.

SOURCE NOTES

Abbreviations:

HFMI—Phatak, N. R., ed. *Mahatma Gandhi: Source Material for a History of the Freedom Movement in India*, vol. 3.
CWMG—*The Collected Works of Mahatma Gandhi*. Ahmedabad: Ministry of Information and Broadcasting, 1965.
SWJN—*Selected Works of Jawaharlal Nehru*, vol. 4. New Delhi: Orient Longman, 1972.
CAS—Oral History, Centre of South Asian Studies, University of Cambridge.

Chapter 1

The imperial train: December 24, 1929, *Times* (London); December 24–25, 1929, *Times of India*.

"We shall have our": "Philosophy of the Bomb," published by the Hindustan Socialist Republican Association, 1930. This was written in response to Gandhi's treatise "The Cult of the Bomb" after the attack on Lord Irwin.

"the glittering jewel": Tharoor, ch. 1.

"Nearly every kind": Ibid.

"Trade, not territory": Collins and LaPiere, 21.

"a company of": Ibid., 22.

Using wile: Ibid., 23.

"breakwaters to the": Ackerman and DuVall, 68.

Second, the British seeded: Ibid.

"loyal opposition": Ibid., 69.

"Though downtrodden": Ibid., 70.

"All my hopes and": Roberts, *The Holy Fox*, 6; The Earl of Halifax, 13–97.

Lord Irwin heard: December 24, 1929 *Times* (London); December 24–25, 1929, *Times of India*.

"Lucky no harm": December, 25, 1929, *Bombay Chronicle*.

"a dastardly outrage": December 24, 1929, *Times of India*.

Chapter 2

Later that same day: December 23, 1929, *Times* (London).

"ugliest man in": Mehta, 3–5.

The two leaders had met: Fischer, 250.

thought Irwin a "good man": Guha, 244.

"Indians were being": Fischer, 250.

Almost three months: Nanda, *The Nehrus*, 316–17.

"general picture of": Dwarkadas, 38–39.

Mohandas Karamchand Gandhi was born: Mehta, 70–73.

A shy, sensitive: Fischer, 12–29; Kripalani, 2–15.

"touch wine, women": Fischer, 35.

At the time, there were: Ackerman and DuVall, 62–63.

Shortly after his arrival: Lelyveld, 3–5.

"You may," Gandhi said: Gandhi, *An Autobiography*, 113.

"His charioteer is": Author Interview with Lisa Trivedi, February 2023.

"A laborer with": Collins and LaPiere, 56–57.

"Declare opposition to": Ackerman and DuVall, 65.

"the means may": Dalton, 17.

"of doing something big": Nanda, *The Nehrus*, 322.

In the northwest: CAS-Oral History, Dhurandhar, B. R.; Slade, 107–8.

The forty-year-old: Shirer, 39.

When Nehru got: Guha, 309.

"Independence means for us": December 30, 1929, *Bombay Chronicle*; December 30, 1929, *Times* (London).

"bomb outrage on": Nayar, 224–25.

At one minute: CAS-Oral History, Deogirikar, T. R.; Reynolds, 26–27.

Chapter 3

At the end of World War I: Guha, 68–73.

On April 6, 1919: Kripalani, 80.

a "Himalayan miscalculation": CWMG 15:436.

But events were: Wagner, 154–83.

"Victory to Mahatma Gandhi": Amin, 2.

"Noncooperation with evil": Guha, 153.

"I am not interested": June 12, 1924, *Young India*.

Then, unpeeling one: Fischer, 245–46.

By the time his train: January 2, 1930, *Young India*.

Gandhi's community: Watson, 44.

After many years: Gandhi and Gandhi, *The Forgotten Woman*, 249–51.

The poet and nationalist: Paranjape, vii–xiii.

"For myself, I delight in warfare": CWMG 44:468.

his "inner voice": Fischer, 264.

One option available: CWMG 42:viii.

Whatever they decided: Slade, 109.

At the ashram, everyone: CAS-Oral History, Nair, C. K.; Chaudhary, 66–67.

Manilal understood the discipline: Gandhi and Gandhi, *The Forgotten Woman*, 121.

"We believe that": Sitaramayya, 363.

"stage lightning and": Gopal, 55.

"Independence will bring": Mitra, 4.

"I shall discharge": Ibid., 22.

was a "childish offer": January 30, 1930, *Young India*.

"Salt," Gandhi said: Paranjape, 235.

"fight of such magnitude": CWMG 42:414.

"Do you expect us all": Slade, 110.

"to the young wives": Morton, 110–17.

The day she and Gandhi met: Polak, Brailsford, and Pethick-Lawrence, 7.

"The only wonder": Roberts and Ash, 51.

a "divine substance": Kurlansky, 3.

caused "unquestioned hardship": Dalton, 99.

"No one seems particularly": Paranjape, 235.

Chapter 4

Lord Irwin deliberately: March 6, 1930, *Bombay Chronicle.*

Gandhi had composed: CAS-Oral History, Dhurandhar, B. R.

"Dear friend," the letter opened: March 7, 1930, *Bombay Chronicle.*

Irwin was left bewildered: Roberts, *"The Holy Fox,"* 18–21; Gopal, 15–17.

"complete severance of": Gopal, 35.

"firm action at the outset": Dalton, 123.

"strike hard and quick": Ibid., 127.

"Upon the supreme": Guha, 326.

"We're not going": March 8, 1930, *Bombay Chronicle.*

"turn out to be": February 15, 1930, *Daily Telegraph.*

"We have begun": Ibid., 125.

"Salt does not appear": Guha, 319.

"His Excellency, the": March 8, 1930, *Daily Telegraph.*

"Next to air": February 27, 1930, *Young India.*

"Satyagraha literally means": Ibid.

Gandhi had experience: Dalton, 101–3; Weber, 88.

"shoot the Indians": *New Statesman*, September 17, 2013.

On March 5, 1930: Remarks at Prayer Meeting, March 5, 1930, CWMG, vol. 43.

a "war unprecedented": Mitra, 28.

"On bended knees": March 12, 1930, *Young India.*

"[May I offer] my": Dalton, 98.

"had gone through": March 12, 1930, *Young India.*

"I must be considerate": Tendulkar, 26.

So too did the distance: Guha, 320. The common assumption is that the route was 240 miles. Thomas Weber, who retraced the route by foot forty years ago, calculated the distance to actually be 220 miles (350 kilometers).

a "damp squib": CAS-Oral History, Narayanswami, C. K.; Nanda, *The Nehrus*, 327.

"It is difficult": Weber, 90.

another "hobby horse": Ibid., 328.

Even Gandhi's long-standing: December 1984, *Gandhi Marg*.

Now, on March 11: Weber, 137–38.

"Either we shall": Speech at Prayer Meeting, Sabarmati Ashram, March 11, 1930, CWMG, vol. 43.

"The fight should continue": Interview with H. D. Rajah, March 11, 1930, CWMG, vol. 43; Interview with the *Manchester Guardian*, March 11, 1930, CWMG, vol. 43.

"In all probability": March 20, 1930, *Young India*.

That night, Gandhi kept: Slade, 111; March 18, 1930, *Bombay Chronicle*; Dhupelia-Mesthrie, 200.

Chapter 5

At 4:00 a.m., the dull clang: March 18, 1930, *Bombay Chronicle*.

Among them was Anand: Weber, 11; https://ramchandanidays.wordpress.com/2014/04/06/anand-t-hingorani-dandi-march/.

So too had Ratnaji: Weber, 16.

"first batch of Satyagrahis": March 12, 1930, *Young India*.

Kasturba understood: I am deeply indebted to Arun and Sunanda Gandhi's wonderful book on Kasturba entitled *The Forgotten Woman: The Untold Story of Kastur, Wife of Mahatma Gandhi*, 251–256.

"We are entering upon": Dalton, 108.

"Do you want": Gandhi and Gandhi, *The Forgotten Woman*, 251–52; Dhupelia-Mesthrie, 201.

Kasturba placed a garland: January 4, 2007, *Al Jazeera*.

"It was an invocation": Ibid.

At last, the Satyagraha Ashram: Dalton, 109.

"Men and women, boys and girls": March 16, 1930, *Pratap*. As quoted from Guha, 321–22.

Lining the road: Weber, 137.

"All our clothes": Basu, 70–71.

Gandhi headed into: March 13, 1930, *Bombay Chronicle*.

"the exodus of Israelites": Tendulkar, 30–31.

"go back and resolve": March 18, 1930, *Bombay Chronicle*.

When the marchers: Weber, 134–44; March 18, 1930, *Bombay Chronicle*.

"It was a perfect": March 18, 1930, *Bombay Chronicle*.

"The soldiers of": Tendulkar, 31.

Over the next several hours: CAS-Oral History, Dhurandhar, B. R.

Chapter 6

The next morning, March 13: March 14, 1930, *Times of India*; March 24, 1930, *Bombay Chronicle*; Weber, 148–154.

"It is of no": Weber, 149.

"If we cannot": Speech at Bareja, March 13, 1930, CWMG, vol. 43.

"The historic march for freedom": March 15, 1930, *Bombay Chronicle*.

"Each hour is important": Circular to PCC, March 12, 1930, SWJN 4:277.

sad, "theatrical" spectacle: March 15, 1930, *Bombay Chronicle*.

"If you look": February 25, 1930, *Bombay Chronicle*.

"The best thing to do": January 1985, *Gandhi Marg*.

It is true that: The Earl of Halifax, 124–40.

"places like this": Bernays, 53.

The easy answer: Hardiman, 191–93.

would be a "fiasco": Weber, 411.

Irwin suspected: Tewari, 151.

He sent sizable: HFMI-Part III, 52–61.

"So, Shankar has": March 20, 1930, *Young India*.

"to make amends": December 1984, *Gandhi Marg Gandhi Peace Foundation*.

"sin of one": "We Are All One," CWMG 43:79–82.

"The unbearable heat of the sun, hot gusts": Weber, 160.

With each step, they: Ibid., 157–95.

The marchers found: March 20, 1930, *Young India*.

The Mahi River, a tidal river: CAS-Oral History, Nair, C. K.; March 21, 1930, *Bombay Chronicle*.

Shortly after midnight: Ibid.

At each stopping placee: HFMI-Part III, 18.

After their discussion: Mitra, 338.

"The time for empty": SWJN 4:287–88.

"Here was the pilgrim": Nanda, *Mahatma Gandhi*, 7.

Chapter 7

One day followed: Weber, 237; CAS-Oral History, Tikekar, S. R.

"God has given him a strong": Letter to Sushila Gandhi, March 14, 1930, CWMG, vol. 43.

"Mussulmans, Parsis, Christians": Speech at Broad, March 26, 1930, CWMG, vol. 43.

In sharp contrast: March 29, 1930, *Bombay Chronicle*.

Self-rule for India: Ibid, 17. In summarizing the philosophy of Gandhi, I am deeply indebted to the insight of Dennis Dalton and his masterpiece *Gandhi's Power: Nonviolence in Action*.

"I propose to make": April 3, 1930, *Young India*.

The day before Gandhi's: March 28, 1930, *Times of India*.

Now forty-three: The Earl of Halifax, 103–5.

"deplorably weak" approach: Roberts, *"The Holy Fox,"* 32.

"dejected on the": HFMI-Part III, 21.

"engaged in a": March 22, 1930, *Daily Telegraph*.

causing "great excitement": Tewari, 152.

"keep the political": Roberts, *"The Holy Fox,"* 32.

In the district: April 4, 1930, *Daily Telegraph*.

"a very happy solution": Tewari, 151.

"situation deteriorated fast": Ibid., 152.

"Although I was": Speech at Delad, March 30, 1930, CWMG 43:157.

On April 1, ten thousand: Weber, 300–301; April 3, 1930, *Times of India*.

"There is no alternative": Speech at Surat, April 1, 1930, CWMG 43:162.

"You shall get": Speech at Prayer Meeting, April 3, 1930, CWMG 43:173.

"right royal reception": Weber, 319.

Most of those: April 7, 1930, *Times of India*.

"Salt suddenly became": Dalton, 113.

Chapter 8

"the murmur of": Weber, 331.

A small bridge crossed: Ibid.

"The red sun": Guha, 329–30.

Set atop hummocks: April 7, 1930, *Times* (London); Guha, 330.

"The 6th of April has been": Statement to *Associated Press*, April 5, 1930, CWMG 43:179.

"I know nothing": April 5, 1930, *Daily Telegraph*.

"As long as the current": April 6, 1930, *Le Journal*.

"I want world sympathy": A Message, April 5, 1930, CWMG 43:180.

If he was arrested: CAS-Oral History, Dhurandhar, B. R.

Nearby, in huts: Weber, 332–33; Guha, 331.

Gandhi emerged from the bungalow: Weber, 334; *Times*, April 7, 1930.

"When I left Sabarmati": Speech at Dandi, April 5, 1930, Dalton, 114.

The next morning, April 6: April 7, 1930, *Times* (London).

Naidu cared not: Nayar, 331–32.

"This religious war": Dalton, 115.

"With this salt": Weber, 348–49; April 7, 1930, *Bombay Chronicle*; April 8, 1930, *Times of India*; April 7, 1930, *Daily Telegraph*; April 7, 1930, *Times* (London); April 9, 1930, *Le Journal*. There are many versions of this event, including dispute over whether Naidu said, "Hail Deliverer." Having examined contemporaneous accounts from journalists on hand on the day, I've concluded that this is what she indeed said.

"Now that a technical": Interview with *Free Press of India*, April 6, 1930, CWMG 43:199.

"The little lawbreaker": Guha, 333.

Chapter 9

"The 6th of April is a": Message to the Punjab Satyagraha Conference, April 6, 1930, SWJN 4:301.

"Lusty cheers rose": April 8, 1930, *Times of India*; April 9, 1930, *Le Journal*.

"I am addressing": Letter from Mahadev Desai to Nehru, April 7, 1930, Nehru, *A Bunch of Old Letters*, 87–88.

These began in Surat: April 8–9, 1930, *Bombay Chronicle*.

Most confrontations with: April 10, 1930, *Young India*.

"Ours is a war": Speech at Aat, April 8, 1930, CWMG 43:21.

"You may arrest": April 17, 1930, *Young India*; Basu, 62.

Still on his travels: Students and Civil Disobedience, April 6, 1930, SWJN 4:300.

"Let all who dare": Statement to the Press, April 8, 1930, SWJN 4:302.

"slow down to die": April 16, 1930, *Daily Telegraph*.

"The real heat": Fragment of Letter to President, BPCC, April 12, 1930, CWMG 43:244.

"If by strength": To the Women of India, April 10, 1930, CWMG 43:219–20.

"We shall have become": Speech at Dandi, April 13, 1930, CWMG 43:252–53.

they must "court suffering": April 14, 1930, *Times of India*.

"Keep smiling, fight": Message to the People, SWJN 4:314.

"It was impossible for the": Appeal to the Youth of India, April 16, 1930, CWMG 43:257–58.

"the symbol of": April 15, 1930. *Bombay Chronicle*.

"wild and woolly": April 23, 1930, *Times of India*.

"There is no doubt": Guha, 337.

Across the country, in cities: April 16, 1930, *Times* (London); April 16, 1930, *Bombay Chronicle*.

"I am anxious": Dalton, 130.

"The policy of": April 12, 1930, *Daily Telegraph*.

"It'd be possible": April 14, 1930, *Times* (London).

"One single man": April 8, 1930, *Le Journal*.

"the Campaign of the Hindu": April 9, 1930, *Le Journal*.

a "saint" and "statesman": March 31, 1930, *Time*.

"This immortal Indian": Holmes, April 27, 1930.

"harms the struggle": Interview with Free Press of India, April 17, 1930, CWMG 43:277.

In Bengal: April 21, 1930, *Times of India*.

"small body of men": April 22, 1930, Ibid.

shoot "unarmed brethren": Gopal, 69–70.

"Gandhi's exemption from": Guha, 337.

"they had already": Tewari, 154.

"I cannot bring": Ibid., 154–55.

Chapter 10

On April 26: April 26, 1930, *Bombay Chronicle*; Speech at Bulsar, April 26, 1930, CWMG 43:327–31.

"Pledged as we": April 24, 1930, *Young India*.

"I am conceiving": Letter to Mirabehn, April 24, 1930, CWMG 43:319.

To manufacture salt, workers: Weber, 342.

"You may call me": Speech at Chharwada, April 26, 1930, CWMG 43:330–32.

Farther down the hillside: February 28, 2015, *The Guardian*.

"The crowds flow": May 2, 1930, *Le Petit Parisien*.

"My country has embarked": Ibid.; April 26, 1930, *Bombay Chronicle*.

the "swirling mob": Sudhir, 132.

"better to die": April 28, 1930, *Bombay Chronicle*.

"only hope that": April 28, 1930, *Times* (London).

"dissemination of sedition": Ibid.

"The day that": Sudhir, 132–33.

"We Englishmen take": April 29, 1930, *Le Journal.*

Irwin hesitated to give: Sudhir, 131–33.

On April 29: Gopal, 70–71.

"This is my last": Speech in Surat, May, 4, 1930, CWMG 43:396–97.

"Dear Friend," he began: Letter to Viceroy, May 4, 1930, CWMG 43:389–92.

It was after midnight: Mazumdar, *Gandhi versus the Empire*, 33–38; May 8, 1930, *Young India*.

"Have you come": Ibid. The dialogue in this section is largely drawn from Muzumdar's account.

The two officials: Weber, 426.

"Any word, Mr. Gandhi?": Farson, 574–77; May 6, 1930, *Daily Telegraph*.

Chapter 11

"The Little State": Letter to Padmaja Nadiu, May 7, 1930, Paranjape, 236.

"Down with the red": May 9, 1930, *Le Petit Parisien.*

"We are the custodians": May 6, 1930, *Bombay Chronicle.*

In the holy city: May 9, 1930, *Le Petit Parisien.*

"For over an hour": Sharp, 123.

"serious nature and": May 15, 1930, *Young India*; May 13, 1930, *Times of India*; CAS-Oral History, Kabadi, S.; Weber, 432–38. This scene is drawn from numerous accounts. These were the foremost.

Behind the old stone: Nayar, 288; Guha, 340.

He kept to a rigid: Weber, 431–32.

Gandhi had "spurned": May 13, 1930, *Bombay Chronicle.*

"seek a friendly": Sharp, 121–23.

But Irwin's view: Ibid., 132.

"keep their heads": May 7, 1930, *Bombay Chronicle.*

Since April 6: HFMI-Part III, 33.

Chapter 12

"What will happen at": Letter to Padmaja Naidu, May 14, 1930, Paranjape, 237.

"The time has come": May 15, 1930, *Bombay Chronicle*.

At the Wadala Salt Works outside: May 19, 1930, *Daily Herald*.

"You are now": May 19, 1930, *Times of India*.

Manilal Gandhi led: Ibid.; May 18–20, *Bombay Chronicle*.

"I wish to talk": May 4, 1956, *Indian Opinion*.

Chapter 13

While volunteers rushed: Letter to Narandas Gandhi, May 18–20, 1930, CWMG 43:417–18.

"I have taken": May 23, 1930, *Bombay Chronicle*.

"the biggest demonstration yet": Miller, 190–92.

Even after sunrise: Ibid., 190–99; Gujarat Provincial Congress Committee, 33–95; Gandhi and Gandhi, 254; June 3, 1930, *Le Petit Parisien*; May 22, 1930, *Times of India*; May 29, 1930, *Young India*; May 5, 1956, *Indian Opinion*; May 22, 1930, *Le Journal*; CAS-Oral History, Batiwala; Tendulkar, 50–51; Sharp, 133–47. The description and quotes from the Dharasana raid were drawn primarily from these sources. In particular, the contemporaneous newspaper accounts from Webb Miller, as well as a pair of French journalists, were particularly helpful.

Chapter 14

"Police forced to": Weber, 448.

"One police officer": May 23, 1930, *Times of India*.

"Your Majesty can": Ashe, 292.

a "mass attack" by: May 23, 1930, *Times of India*.

British censors tried: Miller, 196–99.

"Those who live": Sharp, 157.

The afternoon after: May 29, 1930, *Young India*.

"My one hand": Gujarat Provincial Congress Committee, 85–103.

"Miss Satyagrahi": Guha, 349.

"Mass action": Weber, 457.

The long-awaited report: Tendulkar, 56.

The ingenious strategy: Sudhir, 150–51.

"Time Not Ripe": Leaders' Joint Statement, August 15, 1930, HFMI-Part III, 716.

"I run to mother": Letter to Narandas Gandhi, November 4, 1930, CWMG 44:276.

"God has given him the strength": Letter to Sushila Gandhi, November 16, 1930, CWMG 44:313.

"invaded the classroom": January 12, 1931, *Manchester Guardian*.

"Curiously," *Time*'s editors: January 5, 1931, *Time*.

In January 1931: Guha, 352–57; Prime Minister's Declaration at Round Table Conference, January 19, 1931, CWMG 44:424–25.

"I have come": January 27, 1931, *Times of India*.

Chapter 15

Gandhi was welcomed: January 28, 1931, *Times of India*.

"I want the substance": Ibid.

From Bombay, Gandhi: Letter to Viceroy, February 1, 1931, CWMG 45:136.

"I am going soon": Tendulkar, 66.

"Let us deserve": Message on Motilal Nehru's Death, February 7, 1931, CWMG 45:159.

Motilal Nehru had: Guha, 358.

"I would like to meet": Letter to the Viceroy, February 14, 1931, CWMG 45:175–76.

At 2:15 p.m. on the appointed: February 18, 1931, *Times of India*.

One of the grandest: February 11, 1931, *Times of India*.

"Gandhism and all": Sudhir, 160.

"No one can": Nayar, 316–17.

And despite Gandhi's: Roberts, "*The Holy Fox*," 38.

"Constitutional reform was": The Earl of Halifax, 147–48.

"No Englishman can": Roberts, *"The Holy Fox,"* 42.

Once informed of: February 18, 1931, *Times of India*.

"He seemed to be a": Watson, 62.

Shortly before dusk: February 18, 1931, *Times of India*; February 18, 1931, *Times* (London).

"In my opinion": February 24, 1931, *Times* (London); Fischer, 277; Nayar, 327. There are several versions of this statement. Primarily, I used the one published in the contemporaneous report.

"I will put some": Fischer, 277–78.

"It is all hanging": February 19, 1931, *Times of India*.

"A lot of people found": Roberts, *"The Holy Fox,"* 39.

Steadily, they knocked: Guha, 360–61; Nayar, 328–35.

"Gandhi, you haven't": Tendulkar, 71.

"The Viceroy's Triumph": March 5, 1931, *Bombay Chronicle*.

"His concessions will": Ibid.

"intensified a hundredfold": Sharp, 220.

"Shortly after the talks": Guha, 334.

"there can be no": Sharp, 221.

"For the first time since": Shirer, 46.

"What, then, had Indians": Polak, Brailsford, and Pethick-Lawrence, 188.

"Gandhi showed what": CAS-Oral History, Ali, A.

Chapter 16

"It was a wonderful": Roberts, *"The Holy Fox,"* 43.

"this most remarkable": The Earl of Halifax, 147.

"I shall work": Kripalani, 135.

"to the conscience": Guha, 381.

"So I was": Miller, 236.

Unfortunately, regarding the: Polak, Brailsford, and Pethick-Lawrence, 191.

"Long years ago": McArthur, 234–37.

"get rid of the present": Guha, 757.

"The Mahatma has": Ibid., 850.

"The time is over": "My Father, Do Not Rest": All India Radio broadcast, February 1, 1948.

Manilal Gandhi was in Durban: Manilal Gandhi Memorial Number, April 1956, *Indian Opinion.*

"Complete blankness seems": Ibid., 318.

"It was truly": Dhupelia-Mesthrie, 316.

"that great moment": May 15, 1931, *Indian Opinion.*

"mold heroes out of": Tewari, 107. This is a famous line from Gokhale, quoted in part by Tewari.

Epilogue

"I can say without": Nanda, *Mahatma Gandhi*, 40.

"Gandhi was probably": Ibid., 260.

"disciple of Gandhi": Guha, 883.

"soldiers of its own": Ackerman and DuVall, 494.

"a great man": August 26, 2014, *Hindustan Times.* This quote came from an interview with Nehru conducted by Richard Attenborough, the director of the Oscar-winning film on Gandhi.

History has proven: Chenoweth and Stephan, 6–7.

INDEX

Note: Page numbers in *italics* refer to illustrations.

ACKNOWLEDGMENTS

Writing a book is a solitary journey, especially during a global pandemic, but the support and guidance of numerous individuals along the way make it a truly collaborative endeavor. I extend my heartfelt thanks to those who have played an integral role in the creation of *The Salt March*.

First, kudos to my literary agent, Eric Lupfer, who helped shepherd an idea I had over a decade ago into reality. Eric, your unwavering belief in the potential of this project and your exceptional dedication have been instrumental. I am indebted to my editor, Lisa Sandell; your editorial skills, support, and keen eye for detail have elevated this manuscript to new heights. To the whole team at Scholastic, thank you for your continued support and passion for bringing narrative nonfiction to a younger audience. A special shout-out as always goes to Liz Hudson, whose thoughtful suggestions, rigorous feedback, and unwavering commitment to excellence have transformed my words into a work that I am truly proud of.

I extend my gratitude to two early readers of the manuscript, Thomas Weber and Lisa Trivedi, who generously shared their expert insights and perspectives. Your meticulous attention and constructive criticism have been invaluable.

Thank you to illustrator Mithil Thaker. You've helped bring this story to vivid life. Every time I heard there was a new panel of art, I couldn't wait to see what you had created—and you always managed to surpass my expectations. It's been a great collaboration. To my wife, Diane, and our two daughters, you are my inspiration.

I dedicated this book to librarians. You fostered my early love for books; you've made possible my many works of nonfiction; and most important, you help bring so much wonderful light into a world that may often favor darkness.

Lastly, I would like to express gratitude to my readers. It is your curiosity and thirst for knowledge that motivate authors like myself to continue sharing stories that illuminate our past. May this book spark conversations and contribute to a deeper understanding of our shared history.

NEAL BASCOMB is the author of *The Race of the Century: The Battle to Break the Four-Minute Mile,* which *Kirkus Reviews* called a "gripping narrative nonfiction tale," and *The Nazi Hunters*, winner of the YALSA Award for Excellence in Nonfiction, among numerous other awards. *School Library Journal* praised his second young adult book, *Sabotage*, as "excellent" in a starred review and *The Grand Escape* as a "fantastic pick for avid history readers," also in a starred review. His book *The Racers* was named a *BCCB* Blue Ribbon Book, and in a starred review from *School Library Journal* it was deemed "Highly Recommended." In addition, he is the author of several works of nonfiction for adults on subjects ranging from a 1905 Russian submarine mutiny to a contemporary high school robotics team. *The Perfect Mile*, *Winter Fortress*, and *Hunting Eichmann* went on to be *New York Times* and international bestsellers. Neal lives in Philadelphia with his family and rascal dog, Moses. Please visit his website at nealbascomb.com and follow him on Facebook @nealrbascomb.